Exploring Our Country's History

Literature Bridges to Social Studies Series

Exploring the World of Sports: Linking Fiction to Nonfiction. By Phyllis J. Perry. 1998.

Exploring Our Country's History: Linking Fiction to Nonfiction. By Phyllis J. Perry. 1998.

Exploring Our Country's History

Linking Fiction to Nonfiction

Phyllis J. Perry

Teacher Ideas Press
An Imprint of Greenwood Publishing Group
361 Hanover Street
Portsmouth, New Hampshire
1993

For David

TEACHER IDEAS PRESS
An Imprint of Greenwood Publishing Group
361 Hanover Street
Portsmouth, NH 03801
1-800-225-5800
www.teacherideaspress.com

Production Editor: Kay Mariea
Copy Editor: Jason Cook
Proofreader: Sebastian C. Hayman
Typesetter: Kay Minnis

Library of Congress Cataloging-in-Publication Data

Perry, Phyllis Jean.
    Exploring our country's history : linking fiction to nonfiction /
Phyllis J. Perry.
        xvi, 133 p. 22x28 cm. -- (Literature bridges to social studies series)
    Includes bibliographical references and index.
    ISBN 1-56308-622-0 (pbk.)
    1. United States--History--Juvenile literature--Bibliography.
2. United States--History--Study and teaching--Aids and devices.
3. Historical fiction, American--Juvenile literature--Bibliography.
I. Title. II. Series.
Z1236.P46   1998
[E178.3]
016.973--dc21   98-20275
                                                        CIP
P

Contents

v

Part II
The 1700s

Part III
The 1800s

Part IV
The 1900s

Part V
Additional Resources

About the Series

In this era of literature-based reading programs, students are involved in reading narrative more than ever before, but they still face difficulty when confronted with expository text. Many experts believe that one of the best ways to teach any topic is to engage the learner, that is, to interest students enough so that their motivation to learn about a topic increases.

The Literature Bridges to Social Studies series seeks to use the power of fiction to bring students from the world of imagination into the world of fact. In this series, fiction is used to build interest, increase familiarity with a topic, enlarge background, and introduce vocabulary. The fiction is to be enjoyed, letting the power of the story create a desire to learn more about a topic. A variety of fiction titles should be shared with the class, to suit individual tastes and the breadth of experience in a group of students.

As student interest builds naturally, one or more "bridge" books are used to pique interest in a topical exploration. At this point, the teachers can introduce a main theme of study to the class with confidence that students have developed sufficient background knowledge of that topic. Interest in the topic might then be strong enough to motivate students to attempt the expository writing in nonfiction titles. A collection of poetry is included in each bridge section to broaden reading options.

Just as a variety of fiction titles should be used to introduce a topic, the Literature Bridges to Social Studies series suggests that a variety of nonfiction titles be shared with the class as they begin their topical explorations. Thus, the series is particularly useful to those teachers who are transforming their teaching style to a cross-curricular approach. Nonfiction titles selected for this resource represent the more literary treatments of a topic, in contrast to a textbook-like stream of facts.

Introduction

This book is designed to assist any busy elementary teacher in planning an integrated unit of study involving history. It includes suggestions for individual, small-group, and large-group activities across disciplines. Multiple titles allow for choice based on students' interests and skill levels. The titles, of various lengths and levels of difficulty, were selected from a large number of books recommended by children's librarians. This book is appropriate for teachers of kindergarten through fifth grade.

Between the fiction and nonfiction titles in each part are two suggested "bridge" titles. Bridge titles combine factual information with elements of narrative, such as anecdotes and diary entries. This blend enables the reader to make an easy transition from fiction to nonfiction. Also included in each bridge section is a selection of American history–related poetry.

Parts I, II, III, and IV contain summaries of fiction titles, bridge and poetry titles, and nonfiction titles. For each fiction title, discussion starters and multidisciplinary activities are suggested. For each nonfiction title, topics for further investigation are suggested. These activities involve skills in research, oral and written language, science, math, geography, and the arts.

Each of these parts begins with a "bookweb," which lists all titles included in that part and suggests a variety of related topics to explore. All titles selected for this resource (excluding resources listed in Part V) were published since 1985 and the majority since 1993. All titles are readily available. Many genres are represented.

📖 Teaching Methods 📖

This book is designed to be used in a variety of teaching situations. It may be used by one teacher who is responsible for teaching a number of subjects to a group of students, by teachers in schools where there is departmentalization, and in team teaching situations.

One Teacher with Multiple Teaching Responsibilities

In most cases at the elementary level, a single teacher is responsible for teaching a variety of subjects to a group of students. If the same teacher is responsible for teaching language arts, social studies, math, and science, the multidisciplinary approach suggested in this book will have a unifying effect on the curricula.

Before beginning a unit on some period in American history, the teacher might, for example, read aloud one of the fiction titles in class. This will help set the tone for the upcoming unit of study. As students hear an interesting work of literature dealing with some aspect of American history, they will begin to learn the related vocabulary and to focus on their interest in American history.

The teacher might suggest that students be alert to information about historical events and political figures. Students might be encouraged to bring to class articles that they clip from newspapers and magazines for the beginnings of a classroom vertical file. If a television program, such as a Civil War documentary, will focus on some aspect of American history, the teacher or another student might alert the class to the viewing opportunity or might, with permission, record the broadcast to share in class.

Once the unit of study begins, the teacher might have each student select one of the fiction titles in Part I and then encourage small-group discussions and sharing among those who have read the same book. This will extend reading, listening, and speaking skills.

For the bridge titles, the teacher might want to assist students who are not as comfortable with nonfiction as they are with fiction. Because bridge titles combine elements of narrative or real-life adventure with nonfiction information and facts, they help students make the transition from one type of reading to the other. Students' growing vocabulary and knowledge about the world and exciting historical events will be assets for reading, understanding, and appreciating nonfiction.

The teacher might assign an expository writing assignment related to American history and combine this with a civics assignment to study the systems the various early colonies used to govern themselves. In this way, a student studying the early colonies, for example, will develop skills in researching, writing an informative paper (that explains, for example, the Mayflower Compact), and preparing a bibliography (if appropriate).

In a creative writing assignment, the student might write an original short story from the point of view of a Wampanoag youth who comes to feast and celebrate the harvest with a group of early Pilgrims. A creative writing assignment is an excellent opportunity to introduce plays and poetry related to American history. Students might experiment with writing poetry of their own after reading a collection included in this resource.

Depending upon the books selected, the teacher might also combine social studies with geography. For example, while learning about the time in our history when huge dust storms swept across the central portion of the United States, forcing many farmers—in the midst of a Great Depression—to move to other areas, students might identify on a map the areas discussed.

Departmentalization with Team Planning

In schools where departmentalization is combined with team planning time, the language arts, social studies, math, and science teachers responsible for students in the primary or intermediate grades might plan a segment of time for a unit on American history. The math and science teachers might concentrate on helping students increase their understanding of such topics as distance, speed, gravity, and jet propulsion as students study the 1900s, when astronauts blasted into space. The social studies teacher might discuss the civil rights movement and the central figures and legislation that propelled that movement forward. The language arts teacher might assign reading, research, and writing assignments based on both fiction and nonfiction titles. Panel discussions and oral presentations of material will improve speaking and listening skills, as will puppet shows and dramatic presentations. Specific skills such as skimming, reading for information, note taking, outlining, and using an index or a glossary might also be introduced or reinforced using nonfiction titles.

Some students will find it easy to understand factual information presented pictorially or in graphs and charts in nonfiction titles. For other students, these may be new sources of information. The teacher should explain how to "read" numerical data and might design assignments so that students have an opportunity to construct their own tables and graphs.

Specialists in the school might also be involved. The music teacher might incorporate some patriotic songs. The art teacher might have students study stamp design, then give students an opportunity to design commemorative stamps appropriate for recent historical events. Classroom and hallway bulletin boards might feature the history of the American flag.

If the school has a computer lab, American history-related software and other electronic media might be purchased. Students might play historical computer games, such as *The Oregon Trail*. Students might write their reports for this unit of study using word processing software.

If the media specialist is responsible for teaching research skills to students, the focus might be on using part of an interactive encyclopedia on CD-ROM that features a particular historical event, using a vertical file on significant political figures, or searching an electronic database on historical parks and monuments. The media specialist might designate an "interest" center for videos, magazines, and books in the media center's collection that features American history, and might use interlibrary loans to increase the materials available for this unit of study.

Team Teaching

Where team teaching occurs, the various team members might choose to present their favorite lessons and experiments, based on personal expertise or interest in a new topic. Next, the teachers might map a sequence and time line so that their students will see the connections between their various subject areas. While one teacher is presenting a lesson, colleagues might assist with small-group discussions, science experiments, or supervision in the media center of a group of students involved in small-group or individual research.

Some activities, such as showing films or videos, might be presented to a large group of students. The team members might be responsible for group stations, in which smaller numbers of students are given the opportunity to extend their knowledge.

📖 Culminating Activities 📖

Whatever the configuration of students and teachers, there might well be an opportunity for a special culminating activity for each part of this unit of study. Part I, for example, deals with the 1600s and the establishment of the early colonies. As a culminating activity for Part I, students might plan and prepare a traditional Thanksgiving feast and presentation.

Finding a time in the school schedule to hold the event; securing the cooperation of all teachers and specialists involved; determining which activities to include; planning a schedule for cooking, decorating, making costumes, and rehearsing; designing and writing invitations; securing class volunteers for various committees; securing adult volunteers to help in rehearsal, purchasing supplies, and feast preparation; and so on; will provide ample opportunities for student committees to contribute.

Different culminating activities will come to mind as students become immersed in their reading. For example, as a culminating activity for Part III, students might role-play heroes or ordinary people during the Civil War. The students would imagine themselves living during those chaotic times and determine topics, issues, and scenes to address in a presentation, such as attitudes about emancipating the slaves, the necessity for blockading a port, dealing with family members who are divided between sympathy for the North or the South, taking part in the Battle of Gettysburg, surviving Valley Forge, or being present at the surrender at Appomattox. Students would then perform their presentation for the class or for another group of students. They might design a printed program and select appropriate music for the presentation.

📖 Scope and Sequence 📖

Part I covers the 1600s. Each book deals with some aspect of the earliest European exploration of our country. The fiction titles include picture books and chapter books. The nonfiction titles discuss such figures and topics as the Mayflower settlers, Peter Stuyvesant, the Plymouth Plantation, and the Native Americans of the northeast woodlands.

Part II covers the 1700s. Each book deals with some aspect of the struggle for independence. The fiction titles include picture books and chapter books. The nonfiction titles discuss such figures and topics as Paul Revere, George Washington, Benjamin Franklin, and the Boston Tea Party.

Part III covers the 1800s. Each book deals with some aspect of the westward expansion or the Civil War. The fiction titles include picture books and chapter books. The nonfiction titles discuss such figures and topics as the Oregon Trail, exploration, early railroading, Jesse James, John C. Fremont, Lewis and Clark, Ulysses S. Grant, Robert E. Lee, and Matthew Brady.

Part IV covers the 1900s. Each book explores some aspect of the United States's involvement in major domestic and world affairs of the twentieth century. The fiction titles include picture books and chapter books. The nonfiction titles discuss such figures and topics as World War I, World War II, the Dust Bowl, the Great Depression, Korea, Vietnam, the first moon landing, Franklin D. Roosevelt, John F. Kennedy, and Lyndon Johnson.

Part V is a list of additional resources. Additional fiction and nonfiction titles are included for each part—the 1600s, the 1700s, the 1800s, and the 1900s.

There are also a few suggestions for using audiocassettes.

The 1600s

Part I

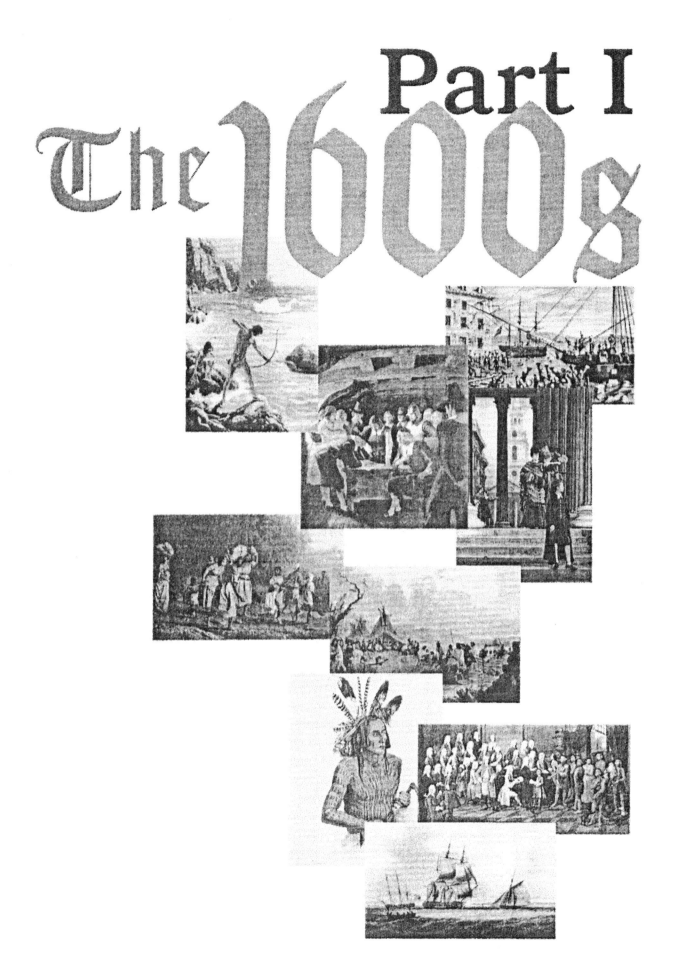

The 1600s

● FICTION ●

- Across the Wide Dark Sea: The Mayflower Journey
- Beyond the Burning Time
- The Mayflower
- Oh, What a Thanksgiving!
- The Seekers
- The Serpent Never Sleeps
- The Story of Squanto, First Friend to the Pilgrims
- This New Land
- Three Young Pilgrims
- Two Chimneys
- When the Great Canoes Came

◆ BRIDGES AND POETRY ◆

- A Journey to the New World: The Diary of Remember Patience Whipple
- Pilgrim Voices: Our First Year in the New World
- A New England Scrapbook: A Journey Through Poetry, Prose and Pictures

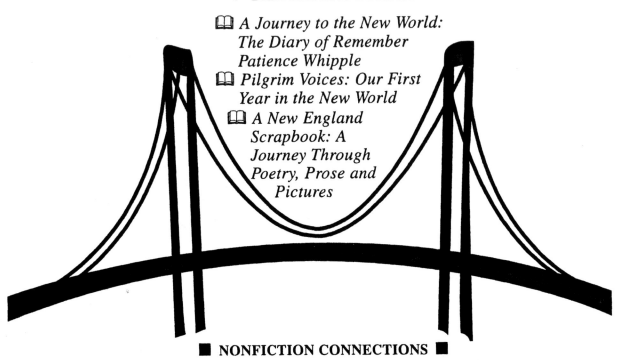

■ NONFICTION CONNECTIONS ■

- Colonial American Craftspeople
- Colonial American Medicine
- Eating the Plates
- Growing Up in Colonial America
- Indians of the Northeast Woodlands
- Making Thirteen Colonies
- The Mayflower People: Triumphs and Tragedies
- Old Silver Leg Takes Over! A Story of Peter Stuyvesant
- Stranded at Plimoth Plantation, 1626
- Tapenum's Day: A Wampanoag Indian Boy in Pilgrim Times
- Thunder from the Clear Sky

—OTHER TOPICS TO EXPLORE—

—Colonial schools	—Indentured servants	—Proprietorships	—Roger Williams
—Dyeing	—New Sweden	—Quakers	—Sailing ships
—Georgia	—Pocahontas	—Rhode Island	—Weaving

The 1600s

● *Fiction* ●

📖 *Across the Wide Dark Sea: The Mayflower Journey*

📖 *Beyond the Burning Time*

📖 *The Mayflower*

📖 *Oh, What a Thanksgiving!*

📖 *The Seekers*

📖 *The Serpent Never Sleeps*

📖 *The Story of Squanto, First Friend to the Pilgrims*

📖 *This New Land*

📖 *Three Young Pilgrims*

📖 *Two Chimneys*

📖 *When the Great Canoes Came*

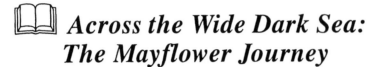

Across the Wide Dark Sea: The Mayflower Journey

by Jean van Leeuwen
illustrated by Thomas B. Allen
New York: Dial Books for Young Readers, 1995. 32p. (unnumbered)

This large-format picture book, filled with soft pastel illustrations, will appeal to students in kindergarten through third grade.

A young boy and his father stand at the ship's railing and watch the shores of England disappear. It is 1620, and this is a sailing ship, the *Mayflower*, heading for America. The ship is tightly packed with almost 100 passengers. It is also packed with tools for building and planting, goods for trading, and guns for hunting. A cat, two dogs, and a few crates of chickens are also on board.

On fair days, the young boy (who narrates the story) stays on deck. He thinks he would enjoy being a sailor. One day, he hears the sailors say that a storm is coming. During the storm, the boy and his brother, mother, and father huddle in the darkness below deck. A man is swept overboard, but he holds tightly to a rope, and the sailors pull him aboard. Another storm damages the ship, but the sailors manage to repair it.

Finally, after nine weeks, land is sighted. A small party goes ashore, followed by the others. The settlers chose to build their shelter high on a hill. The winter is harsh, and sickness is rampant. Half of the settlers die, but those who survive the winter make peace with the Native Americans, begin to farm, and establish their homes in the new land.

Discussion Starters and Multidisciplinary Activities

1 Have students describe how they would feel if they, like the young boy in this story, were standing ashore in the New World in the spring, watching the *Mayflower* turn and head back toward England.

2 The boy's mother brought vegetable seeds to plant in the new land. Invite students to discuss what seeds they would take with them to a new country, and why they would choose these seeds.

3 Have students discuss whether they would be more frightened about crossing the sea to reach a new land or trying to survive and build a settlement in the new land. Why?

4 Ask a group of students to write and illustrate a book, similar in format to *Across the Wide Dark Sea*, about Squanto's voyage to England, how he felt, and what he saw.

5 Help students learn more about seeds by engaging them in an experiment to determine the best conditions for growing healthy plants. Have students plant similar seeds (such as lima beans) in different depths of soil and provide varying amounts of water and exposure to sunlight.

6 The mother in this story planted onions. Have students study plants to observe their cellular and chemical characteristics: On a table, set up a microscope with 50X magnification. Put a piece of onion skin on a glass slide and add one drop of water. Place a cover slip over the onion skin and water and have students examine the onion skin under the microscope. Students will observe box-shaped cells. Have students observe other plants and leaves. Students should look for the tiny green parts of the cells that contain chlorophyll, which gives plants their color.

📖 *Beyond the Burning Time*

FICTION

by Kathryn Lasky

New York: Scholastic; Blue Sky Press, 1994. 273p.

This story, set in 1691, will appeal to fourth- and fifth-grade readers. The book is not illustrated. The central character, Mary Chase, is 12 years old.

As the story begins, Mary is walking home in darkness after having visited her brother in the Salem shipyards. Mary is glad that she didn't join a group of girls who visited Tituba's kitchen to take part in fortune telling. Many of these girls are now behaving strangely.

A doctor comes to Salem and says that "the evil hand" is upon them. Mary does not believe in witches, but she is worried about what might happen as she and her mother, Virginia, try to manage their farm alone. Ministers from several areas are brought to Salem to help, but the shrieking girls disrupt church services.

Afterwards, the girls name three witches: Tituba, Sarah Good, and Sarah Osburne. The women are arrested and questioned in the meetinghouse. All of them deny being witches, but all are imprisoned. In the days that follow, more and more women, and a few men, are arrested for witchcraft. They are tried and executed.

Then Virginia Chase, Mary's mother, is arrested. As she awaits hanging, Mary and her brother, Caleb, work together to save their mother. They plan an escape and rescue her on the day of the hanging, taking her to the river where Eli Coatsworth awaits to give them passage aboard his ship. Mary and her family do not return until years later, after the witchcraft madness has ended.

Discussion Starters and Multidisciplinary Activities

1   Have students discuss why they think Tituba and Sarah Good were the first women in Salem to be accused of witchcraft. Why were these women easy targets?

2   According to Mary Warren, the witchcraft tragedy began "just as sport." Discuss with students events they know of that began innocently but escalated to become hurtful. How does this happen?

3   Although Virginia and Mary Chase were gentle people, they became violent. Virginia attacks her accusers in court. Mary says that she is willing to commit murder to save her mother. Have students discuss this change. What caused it? Were the change and accompanying actions justified?

4   Caleb loved to work with wood, and Mary greatly admired the things that Caleb made. If possible, invite a woodcarver from the community to visit the class, discuss woodcarving, and show students some of the tools used. After the visit, have students send thank you letters to the guest.

5   Some people likened the McCarthy hearings in the 1950s to a witch hunt. Have a small group of interested students work with a media specialist to research the McCarthy hearings. Have the students discuss with the class the similarities between these hearings and the Salem witch trials.

6   Invite students to illustrate a scene from the book using media of their choice, identifying the page where the illustration should be placed. Post the illustrations in the classroom.

 *The Mayflower*

by Kate Waters
photographs by Russ Kendall
New York: Scholastic, 1996. 40p.

FICTION

Students in kindergarten through third grade will enjoy this picture book with a brief narration and engaging full-color photographs.

This story traces the journey of the *Mayflower*, which left England on September 6, 1620, and sailed across the Atlantic Ocean. On board were the ship's master, Christopher Jones, about 30 officers and sailors, and 102 passengers. William Small (an imaginary character), the ship's apprentice, is beginning a seven-year apprenticeship to learn the craft of a mariner and all the navigation skills needed to sail a ship. Also on board is Ellen Moore, a young girl sailing without her family (Ellen Moore actually sailed on the *Mayflower*).

Will begins to learn the skills of a sailor. He is lonely for his family and makes friends with Ellen. The two talk together often, commiserate about rough weather and leaks, and speculate about what it will be like in the New World. After landing in Massachusetts and spending several months there, Will sails back to England, leaving Ellen behind.

The photographs in this book were taken on the *Mayflower II*, a reproduction of what historians think the original *Mayflower* looked like. The *Mayflower II* was built in England using the same methods that would have been used in the seventeenth century and is now on exhibit in Plymouth, Massachusetts.

Discussion Starters and Multidisciplinary Activities

1. Have students discuss what it might have been like to be Will or Ellen, sailing without any family members to the New World. What would cause fear and worry?

2. The crew stayed on deck, where it was dangerous during storms but where there was comfortable space and fresh air. The passengers stayed below, a safer place, but in cramped quarters. Ask students whether they would prefer being a passenger or a crew member on the *Mayflower*.

3. Ask students to discuss how they think Will and Ellen felt when they said good-bye in Massachusetts and Will sailed to England.

4. Ask a pair of interested students, with the help of an adult volunteer, to construct a crossword puzzle using some of the words and definitions that appear on page 40 of the book. Make copies of the puzzle for classmates to solve.

5. There is a detailed diagram of the *Mayflower* on page 37 of the book. Ask a pair of interested students to draw the ship as a large chart, labeling and naming the 12 major areas of the ship. Post the chart on a classroom bulletin board.

6. Although historians are not certain, the *Mayflower* may have flown pennants as well as a flag of the cross of Saint George, a red cross on a white background. Saint George is the patron saint of England. Invite a small group of interested students to research this topic. They should draw the flag, research Saint George and his life, and write a report to share with the class.

 *Oh, What a Thanksgiving!*

FICTION

by Steven Kroll
illustrated by S. D. Shindler
New York: Scholastic, 1988. 32p.

This picture book with full-color illustrations will appeal to students in kindergarten through third grade. The story weaves together past and present Thanksgiving traditions.

David, the main character, has a remarkable imagination. When his teacher, Mr. Sanderson, describes the first Thanksgiving, David imagines the event and wishes that he could have been there to meet Miles Standish and Chief Massasoit.

When his father takes him shopping for Thanksgiving supplies, David thinks about how exciting it would be to hunt for a turkey instead of buying one at a supermarket. When they select two kinds of cranberry sauce, David points out that the Pilgrims didn't have cranberry sauce.

At home, David complains to his mother that their celebration won't be a *real* Thanksgiving. The next morning, while watching the Macy's Thanksgiving parade on television, David imagines a real Thanksgiving parade—the Native Americans and Pilgrims coming to the tables, laden with food.

The family walks to Grandma's house. Partway there, David's mother realizes that they've forgotten something, and David returns home to get it. On the way, he sees Mr. Sanderson standing on a hill. Mr. Sanderson reminds David that people today give thanks for the same things for which the Pilgrims gave thanks. With new understanding, David goes to Grandma's house and has a great Thanksgiving.

Discussion Starters and Multidisciplinary Activities

1   After hearing about Pilgrims in school, David pretends that the school bus he rides is the *Mayflower*, and that when he steps off the bus, he's landing on the shores of the New World. Ask students if they have ever imagined an historic adventure. Allow students to discuss their imagined adventures, if desired.

2   Have students look at the illustrations in the book that depict the clothing worn by Pilgrim children. Ask students whether they prefer Pilgrim-style or modern clothing. Why?

3   The author points out that even baby Katherine "wasn't so bad" at the Thanksgiving dinner. Ask students to share funny experiences involving a baby or small child at a dinner celebration.

4   Have students develop their graphing skills: Ask them to suggest vegetables that might be served at Thanksgiving dinner. Draw a graph on the chalkboard, listing the vegetables along the horizontal axis and numerals along the vertical axis. Have students vote, individually, for their favorite vegetable, keeping a tally on the graph. Which vegetable is the most popular?

5   Several Native American tribes were mentioned in the story. Ask pairs of students to research Massasoit, Squanto, and Samoset and share what they learn with the class.

6   Helping a new friend feel at ease is an art. Have pairs of students pretend to be David and Michael, sitting beside each other at a table. What would each say to the other?

 ## *The Seekers*

FICTION

by Eilis Dillon
New York: Charles Scribner's Sons, 1986. 136p.

Fourth- and fifth-grade readers will enjoy this book told in the first person by 16-year-old Edward Deane. Except for the cover, the book has no illustrations.

The story begins in 1621 in the North of England. Edward expects to remain in this part of the world forever. In time, he hopes to marry his longtime friend Rebecca. Another friend, Andrew Hogdon, is 19 and eager to travel and see the world.

Rebecca's father, Moses, announces that he will take her and his sister, Abigail, across the sea to New England. Edward and Andrew, using money Andrew has saved, book passage on the same boat as Rebecca and her family. On board, Edward and Andrew meet Jack, Stephen, and Kate Cutler. Jack and Stephen Cutler are traders and have sailed back and forth across the sea several times.

On shore, Edward arranges for his group to stay with the Clarks in their home. Edward works as a shipbuilder, and Rebecca helps in the kitchen, until both are asked to teach school. Andrew goes hunting with the Cutlers. Rebecca's father goes to live in the woods because he thinks that he is forced to work too hard with the Clarks. Aunt Abigail tends to the sick.

Fevers strike the settlement, and the winters are harsh. With Abigail's help, though, everyone living with the Clarks survives. Edward and Rebecca decide to return home to England, where they feel they belong. The others begin to thrive and enjoy this new world.

Discussion Starters and Multidisciplinary Activities

1 The two characters who change the most during the course of the story are Moses and Aunt Abigail. Have students discuss each character's changes and the causes.

2 Have students discuss the problems these early settlers faced in New Plymouth. Which was most difficult to overcome?

3 Ask students to explain the reasons Edward and Rebecca had for leaving New Plymouth and returning to England. Were they "weaklings" for leaving?

4 The insulating properties of clothing were important to settlers. Help students conduct an experiment to determine what materials are effective insulators: With supervision, have students fill each of four jars with 1 pint of boiling water (100°C). Place an immersion lab thermometer into each jar and close the jars with lids. Leave one jar unwrapped, wrap one jar in wool, one in cotton, and one in a piece of thermal cloth. Enclose each jar in a plastic bag and put them into a refrigerator. Record the temperature every 15 minutes for two hours. Have students discuss what they learned.

5 Some passengers on the *Swallow* ate lemons daily. Have a group of students research scurvy, what causes it, and why lemons might or might not prevent this disease. Have students share with the class what they learn.

6 Some people in New Plymouth were known as the Saints. Have a group of students research the tenets of their religion. Why did they come to the New World? In an oral report, have students share with the class what they learn.

📖 *The Serpent Never Sleeps*

FICTION

by Scott O'Dell
Boston: Houghton Mifflin, 1987. 227p.

This book is appropriate for students in grades four and five. The central character is 19-year-old Serena Lynn. The text is supplemented with a few black-and-white illustrations.

Serena works at Foxcroft Castle. She meets King James, who offers her a position writing letters for his wife. Before Serena has the opportunity to pursue this offer, Anthony Foxcroft accidentally kills a man at a party in the castle and flees to avoid imprisonment, again. He decides to go to the New World, and Serena decides to follow him.

In 1609, they set sail from Plymouth, England, on the *Sea Venture*, bound for the New World. The ship is bearing colonists and supplies for the settlement at Jamestown.

One of Anthony's enemies is on board; when he discovers Anthony, Anthony is chained and isolated.

When the *Sea Venture* shipwrecks on Bermuda, Serena manages to free Anthony. He volunteers to sail with a group of men for Virginia, but the small boat and the men become lost in a storm.

The settlers leave Bermuda and sail for Virginia. Supplies of food are dangerously low, and Serena is sent on a mission to convince Pocahontas to protect the settlers and to provide them with corn. Serena becomes friends with Pocahontas and marries Tom Barlow. Pocahontas marries John Rolfe. The settlers thrive, but Pocahontas, her husband, and her child travel to England. Pocahontas dies tragically there.

Discussion Starters and Multidisciplinary Activities

1   Have students discuss what they thought when they read that Anthony Foxcroft disappeared at sea. Did they think he was dead? Why? Did they think he would appear later in the story? Why?

2   No one was enthusiastic about sending Serena on a mission to bring Pocahontas to Jamestown. Serena finally slipped away from the boat and acted of her own will. Have students discuss her actions. Was she wise to do what she did?

3   Toward the end of the story, Serena throws her serpent ring into the fire. Have students discuss why they think she did this.

4   The minister in the story uses the new version of the Bible, the King James version. Have students research the King James version of the Bible. Is it still used? Is there a more recent version? What are the differences between versions?

5   Students who especially enjoyed the part of the book about Pocahontas might enjoy reading another book by Scott O'Dell with a Native American maiden as a central character, *Streams to the River, River to the Seas: A Novel of Sacagawea*. Have students discuss both books and share what they liked about each.

6   The shipwreck left the settlers on the island of Bermuda, which some did not want to leave. How is Bermuda different today? Have a group of students contact several local travel agencies and ask for brochures. Post the brochures on a classroom bulletin board.

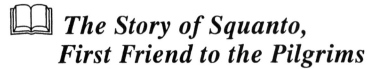

The Story of Squanto, First Friend to the Pilgrims

FICTION

by Cathy East Dubowski
illustrated by Steven James Petruccio
New York: Dell, 1990. 91p.

This book is appropriate for third- through fifth-grade students. The story is told in the third person from the viewpoint of a young Native American boy named Tisquantum. Black-and-white illustrations complement each chapter.

Tisquantum lives with the Wampanoag tribe in Patuxet. When he and others of his tribe are captured by a group of white men and taken to Malaga, Spain, some are sold as slaves and others are rescued by Catholic monks.

After being rescued, Tisquantum lives in London and learns to speak English, then goes to Newfoundland to work as a translator. There, he meets Captain Dermer, with whom he returns to Patuxet. When he reaches his village, Tisquantum learns that his people have died of a plague.

Tisquantum is captured by Chief Massasoit. In November 1620, the *Mayflower* lands at Cape Cod. The following spring Massasoit, wanting the Native Americans and the white settlers to live at peace, sends Samoset to the settlement. He is well-received, and Massasoit sends Tisquantum with Samoset. Tisquantum is called Squanto by the settlers and helps draft a peace treaty.

Squanto becomes a friend to the Pilgrims, whom he teaches and helps. When jealousy arises between Hobbamock and Squanto, Squanto is accused of false dealings, and Massasoit threatens to kill him. The Pilgrims protect Squanto, who lives in the settlement the rest of his life.

Discussion Starters and Multidisciplinary Activities

1 Ask students to discuss what traits Tisquantum developed as a boy that helped him survive when he was captured and taken to Spain and England.

2 As a grown man, Squanto is not completely comfortable with either the Pilgrims or the Native Americans. Have students discuss this.

3 It is not clear whether Hobbamock or Squanto was causing the trouble. Have students discuss the jealousy that grew between them and the problems it caused.

4 Squanto taught the settlers that fertilizer would help them grow a healthy crop of corn. Have students conduct a simple science experiment: Purchase four flowering plants in small pots. Select plants that are as close in size as possible. Put the plants in a sunny window and water as needed. Water two plants with water in which liquid fertilizer has been added. Water the other two plants with tap water. Mark the two pots that are receiving fertilizer. After several weeks, ask students if they can see any differences. Are the fertilized plants larger? Do they appear to be healthier?

5 When Winslow and Hopkins went to see Massasoit, they couldn't sleep at night because of his low singing. Have a music specialist locate authentic Native American music on audiocassette record, or compact disc and share it with the class.

6 Leaving England, the passengers aboard the *Mayflower* numbered 50 men, 20 women, and 32 children. During the first winter in the New World, 50 people died—16 women, 31 men, and 3 children. Have students construct a graph showing survival rates in these three categories.

📖 *This New Land*

by G. Clifton Wisler
New York: Walker, 1987. 124p.

FICTION

Part of the American History Series for Young People, this book will appeal to fourth- and fifth-grade readers. The story is told in the first person from the viewpoint of 12-year-old Richard Woodley. There are no illustrations.

Richard is born in Holland, where his parents had fled with their daughter, Mary, to avoid religious persecution in England. The Woodleys work hard in Holland but are eager to leave and make a better life for themselves in America.

With other passengers, Richard and his family sail in cramped quarters aboard the *Mayflower*. Passengers include both Saints and Strangers. Before landing in Cape Cod, the men sign the Mayflower Compact, agreeing to work together for the common good. They decide to make their settlement in an area they name Plymouth.

The early months in the new land bring much hardship. The Pilgrims must wade through icy waters between the small boats and shore. Storms soak all those still aboard the *Mayflower*. Many become ill and die, including Richard's mother.

These early settlers struggle to find food and to build their first shelters. Those who survive the hardships of winter work even harder in the spring. Homes and a fortress are built. Seeds are planted. The settlers practice with muskets to display their strength to the Native Americans. With the help of friendly natives, the settlers prosper, hold a feast of Thanksgiving with the Indians, and look forward to their new lives in a new land.

Discussion Starters and Multidisciplinary Activities

1. Have students who have read the book, told from the viewpoint of a 12-year-old boy, as well as the bridge book *A Journey to the New World* (see p. 16), told from the viewpoint of a 12-year-old girl in diary format, and compare the two books. Which was most enjoyable? Why?

2. Many careers seem possible for Richard: seaman, carpenter, farmer, soldier, and interpreter between the settlers and the Native Americans. Have students discuss which career they think Richard will choose.

3. Richard's sister, Mary, is 17 when the story begins. Have students discuss the many ways in which her life is different from that of a modern teenage girl.

4. The Pilgrims dried much of the corn that they harvested. Have students conduct an interesting dehydration experiment using apples: Weigh two apples together on a scale and record the weight. With supervision, have students slice the apples thinly and spread the slices on a plate. After leaving the apple slices in a sunny spot for three days, weigh them together. How much less in weight are the dried slices than the original weight of the two apples?

5. Shellfish, such as mussels, sometimes made the settlers ill. Ask a pair of students to research this. Are there times of the year when Atlantic Coast shellfish should not be eaten? Why? Have the students share with the class what they learn.

6. Invite a pair of students, with the help of a media specialist, to find books that have pictures of the Pilgrims' departure site in England and their landing site in what would become Plymouth. Have the students photocopy these pictures (if copyright allows) and share them with the class or show the photographs to the class.

 **Three Young Pilgrims**

by Cheryl Harness
New York: Bradbury Press, 1992. 38p. (unnumbered)

 FICTION

This large-format book with full-color illustrations will appeal to students in kindergarten through third grade. The book opens upon a humorous and colorful map tracing the *Mayflower*'s journey across the Atlantic.

The reader learns that among the 102 passengers leaving Plymouth, England, for America on September 6, 1620, three children are present: Mary, Remember, and Bartholomew. During the journey, the children constantly look for mermaids and pirates, but most of all, they look for land. A two-page spread shows, in a cut-away drawing, where the people, supplies, and cargo are stored on the ship.

After 60 days, land is sighted. The Pilgrims go ashore but continue to spend their nights on the *Mayflower*. By day, the men search for the best location to build their new homes. Just before Christmas, they decide where to build their colony, called Plymouth. Many of the Pilgrims become sick. That winter, half of them die, including the mother of the three children and her new baby.

In the spring, Squanto and Samoset come to the settlement and teach the Pilgrims how to plant corn. The Pilgrims harvest a rich crop and invite the Indians to celebrate with them and offer prayers of thanks—the first Thanksgiving.

Ships arrive with more settlers. The colony grows and the land becomes more fertile. The father of the three children eventually remarries, Bartholomew returns to England, Remember marries and moves to Salem, and Mary settles in Plymouth.

Discussion Starters and Multidisciplinary Activities

1 Have students discuss what the three children might have done to pass the time during their 60 days on the ship. Most of the time, they were not allowed on deck.

2 The first Thanksgiving was special. Invite students to discuss their Thanksgiving holidays. Do relatives and friends come to visit? Do students travel to visit family?

3 When, at the first Thanksgiving, the father of the children asks them whether they are glad they came to the new land, no one answers with a simple "yes" or "no." Have students discuss how they think each of the children felt, and why.

4 The people on shore who watched the *Mayflower* set sail and return to the Old World must have experienced mixed emotions. Half the original settlers had already died in this new land. Invite students to write poems describing the emotions the Pilgrims must have felt at this moment. Post the poems on a classroom bulletin board.

5 The labeled drawing of the *Mayflower* helps the reader imagine the journey. Invite a pair of students to make a similar, enlarged diagram and post it on a classroom bulletin board.

6 Many terms related to sailing vessels are introduced in the book, including *mizzen mast, binnacle, tiller, whipstaff, ballast, keel, capstan, forecastle, anchor windlass, hatch, longboat, beak, crow's nest,* and *main topsail*. Invite a small group of students to make a crossword puzzle using some of these terms, including clues or definitions and an answer key. Photocopy the puzzle for the class to solve.

 *Two Chimneys*

FICTION

by Mary Z. Holmes
illustrated by Geri Strigenz
Austin, TX: Raintree Steck-Vaughn, 1992. 48p.

This book will appeal to readers in grades three and four. Color illustrations complement the text.

Katherine Eastwood, the main character, arrives in Virginia in 1622, when she is seven years old. The family stays in Jamestown until Katherine's father, William, moves them upriver to their land, which they name Eastwood Plantation.

The family begins work on their house, but sickness strikes—Katherine's little brother and her older sister die. Land is cleared for tobacco and food crops. The servants build a cottage, house, warehouse, and wharf. As years pass, Katherine acts like a tomboy, and her mother despairs of turning her into a lady.

When Katherine's brother, Robert, arrives from England, he brings with him a friend, Edward Hollyman, supplies, and also bricks for chimneys for the new house. He brings presents, including a picture of Dudley Newton. Katherine learns that her parents plan to send her to England in a few years and arrange a marriage between her and Dudley.

Robert becomes ill but is nursed back to health. Word comes that his cousin has died, and his uncle is making him heir to the lands he owns, so Robert returns and William decides that Katherine can remain in Virginia. In time, Robert marries and has a child, and Katherine agrees to marry Edward Hollyman and make a home in Virginia.

Discussion Starters and Multidisciplinary Activities

1. Katherine and her brother, Robert, have different feelings about Virginia. Have students discuss this. Why does Katherine love Virginia? Why would Robert rather die than stay in Virginia?

2. Have students discuss why they think that a new house with wooden floors and two chimneys is so important to Katherine's mother.

3. Mercey becomes ill with a high fever and is sick for many days. Katherine brings a little duckling inside and places it on Mercey's bed. Have students discuss this action. Why did Katherine give Mercey a duck?

4. Katherine misses her grandmother, often remembering times they were together in England. Have students write a letter from Katherine to her grandmother about life in the colonies, including details from the book.

5. Katherine's father planted tobacco in Virginia. Invite a small group of students to research tobacco. In which southern states is tobacco still a big cash crop? Which state produces the most tobacco each year? How much? Have the students share what they learn with the class.

6. Robert undertakes the ordeal of bringing a horse to the colonies, but the horse plays almost no role in the story. Ask interested students to add a chapter to the book in which the horse plays a major role. Allow students to share their chapters, if desired.

When the Great Canoes Came

FICTION

by Mary Louise Clifford
illustrated by Joyce Haynes
Gretna, LA: Pelican, 1993. 144p.

This book will appeal to fourth- and fifth-graders. Black-and-white illustrations are included. The story is narrated by an old Native American queen, Cockacoeske, who describes the early settlements in the New World.

Lost Owl is a young Native American boy. There are no priests left to take the young boys into the forest for a *huskenaw* to test them for courage and endurance and to teach them the laws of their people. Lost Owl asks the old queen, Cockacoeske, to tell him and three of his friends the history of their people.

Queen Cockacoeske tells the youths about the creator, Ahone, and about how he gave the people the land and the sea as well as a spirit named Okee to dwell within them. In these early times, there was plenty of food, and many tribes in the area lived together in peace. In 1560, the Spanish came. When they left, they took Opechancanough, a young Native American boy, with them. He was gone 14 years, until he persuaded the Spanish priests, who hoped to convert the Native Americans to Catholicism, to return him to his home.

Opechancanough was welcomed home by his tribe, who eventually killed the priests. After that, many skirmishes occurred. One of the leaders, Powhowtan, tried to reconcile the hostilities with the white people, but Opechancanough wanted to kill them while there were only a few of them. Eventually, the tribes were driven off their lands by the increasing number of white settlers.

Discussion Starters and Multidisciplinary Activities

1 The old woman, Anne, and the old queen, Cockacoeske, sit together as the queen tells her story. In many stories about Native Americans, the old men pass down the history and wisdom. Ask students how having a female narrator affects the story.

2 When the story ends, Lost Owl has run away. Have students discuss what they think he will do and what might happen to him.

3 The queen's son, John West, does a number of evil things in the course of the story. Have students point out what he does and discuss his motivations.

4 Opechancanough was gone so long, many must have thought he was dead. Ask students to write and share a thanksgiving prayer that might have been given at his welcome home ceremony.

5 Have two students conduct a scientific experiment to test short-term memory: First, they should prepare a poster with pictures of 20 objects related to the story (e.g., sailing vessel, canoe, deer, pottery, animal-skin robe, etc.). This poster should not be shared with the class while the students are making it.

Have classmates sit in a circle. The two students should reveal the poster and allow classmates 15 seconds to study it. Have classmates return to their seats and write down the names of as many objects as they can remember. What is the average number of items remembered? Is there a difference in short-term memory between boys and girls? Did those who read the book score higher than those who didn't?

6 To supplement the illustrations in the book, ask interested students to make a black-and-white illustration of their favorite scene from the story, identifying the page where the illustration should be placed. Post the illustrations in the classroom.

◆ *Bridges and Poetry* ◆

 A Journey to the New World: The Diary of Remember Patience Whipple

Pilgrim Voices: Our First Year in the New World

A New England Scrapbook: A Journey Through Poetry, Prose and Pictures

A Journey to the New World: The Diary of Remember Patience Whipple

◆ BRIDGES AND POETRY

by Kathryn Lasky
New York: Scholastic, 1996. 173p.

This bridge book is a work of fiction presented as the diary of a 12-year-old girl, Remember Patience Whipple. It will appeal to third- through fifth-grade readers.

The story begins on the morning of October 1, 1620. Mem (short for Remember) makes a diary entry stating that she, her friend Hummy, and other Saints are journeying to the New World on the *Mayflower*. Mem describes being seasick and the crowded conditions aboard the ship. A rogue wave cracks the main beam of the ship, but the men repair it. Many become ill, and Will, a friend of Mem's, dies.

They land not in Virginia, where they expected to arrive, but in Cape Cod. Once ashore, the men explore, the children play, and the women do the washing. After exploration, the men decide to move the ship to a spot they have named Plimoth and make their settlement there.

The settlers build and hunt all winter. By spring, half have died, including Mem's mother. Samoset and Squanto, Native Americans who speak English, come to their settlement and a peace treaty is drafted between the settlers and the Native Americans.

Hummy returns to England with her father, and Mem endures the sorrow of being without her mother and her best friend. Her father eventually remarries, Mem survives a serious illness, and the settlers and Indians celebrate the first Thanksgiving.

Possible Topics for Further Investigation

1. Corn was important to the Plimoth settlers. Have students experiment with planting corn to determine if the depth at which the seeds are placed affects their growth: Place small rocks into a small aquarium to a depth of 2 inches. Cover the rocks with 2 inches of sand, then add 8 inches of potting soil. Plant 16 corn seeds about 1 inch apart in the aquarium—four seeds at a depth of 1 inch, four seeds at a depth of 2 inches, four seeds at a depth of 3 inches, and four seeds at a depth of 6 inches. Put all the seeds near a glass wall of the aquarium and cover the outside glass wall of the aquarium with black paper. Water as needed. Remove the paper and check the seeds each day. What planting depth produces the healthiest plants?

2. Ask students to role-play the original settlers living in Plimoth. Some will want to be Saints and some will want to be Strangers. Invite students to draft a one-page Mayflower Compact, suggesting rules to live by in the New World. They should not write the compact until general agreement is reached. Compare the students' compact with the real compact.

3. Invite a small group of students to research Squanto, Samoset, and Massasoit. Ask them to list complete information on each of their sources of information. In an oral report, have the students share what they learn with the class.

📖 *Pilgrim Voices: Our First Year in the New World*

◆ **BRIDGES AND POETRY**

edited by Connie Roop and Peter Roop
illustrated by Shelley Pritchett
New York: Walker, 1996. 48p.

This book serves as a bridge because it is presented in the form of actual writings of Pilgrims who settled in the New World. Their story is told from notes and original text dating back to 1622. Full-color illustrations complement the text. This book will appeal to students in grades two through four.

A foreword to the book explains that the story of the Plymouth colony begins about 1606 when a group of English people in Nottinghamshire form an independent church. These Separatists fled in 1609 to the Netherlands to escape religious persecution. In 1620, they decided to colonize the northern parts of Virginia and so set sail on the *Mayflower*.

The remainder of the book is in the form of diary entries covering the ocean voyage, landing parties, exploration of the new land, and finding corn, which the settlers plant and cultivate as their first crop. On December 19, 1620, the settlers decide upon a place to settle and begin the process of felling timber for building. The cold weather makes building slow and difficult. Many of the Pilgrims become ill; about half die during the first winter.

In March, a friendly Indian, Samoset, who speaks some English, comes to the settlement. Through his efforts, a peace treaty is drafted between the English settlers and Massasoit. The little colony begins to thrive, and none of the original Pilgrims choose to return to England the following year.

Possible Topics for Further Investigation

1. Although the Pilgrims were afraid to remain in England because it was treason for them to separate from the Church of England, they still began their formal documents by referring to themselves as loyal subjects of King James. Have a group of students work with an adult volunteer or a media specialist to research King James and the Church of England. When did King James reign? Why was the Church of England so important to him? Were there others that were trying to separate from the church? In an oral report, have the students share with the class what they learn.

2. The Pilgrims sailed from Southampton, England, for Cape Cod in America. Invite a pair of students to research this long journey. On a map, have them locate the starting and ending points and trace the route taken. How many miles did the Pilgrims journey? What was their average distance completed each day? What powered the *Mayflower*? Have the students share with the class what they learn.

3. The final entry, November 9, 1621, states that 35 men have landed at Cape Cope, some eight or ten leagues from the original Pilgrims. Invite students to write additional diary entries, using the format in the book as a model, describing the meeting of the two groups. Will the new group come to live with the original Pilgrims, or will they build a settlement of their own? What problems will arise between the two groups? How will the new group interact with the original group? With the Native Americans? Post the diary entries on a classroom bulletin board.

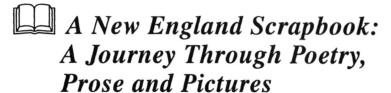

A New England Scrapbook: A Journey Through Poetry, Prose and Pictures

BRIDGES
AND POETRY

by Loretta Krupinski
New York: HarperCollins, 1994. 40p. (unnumbered)

This book with full-color illustrations will appeal to all elementary grades. The pictures, poetry, and prose present the beauty of the states of Maine, Vermont, New Hampshire, Massachusetts, Connecticut, and Rhode Island.

The format of the book involves information about some aspect of New England (e.g., houses), followed by a poem about the topic ("Houses"), followed by a full-page colored drawing (an old house in a country setting).

Topics addressed include old stone walls, maple syrup, rocky shores, old houses, islands, barns, lobster, mountains, Thanksgiving, fog, cranberries, lighthouses, and the four seasons.

Poems include "Stone Wall" by Ann Turner; "Maple Feast" by Frances Frost; "The Sea" (anonymous); "Houses," "Islands," and "I'd Like to Be a Lighthouse" by Rachel Field; "In the Barnyard" by Dorothy Aldis; "The Lobsters and the Fiddler Crab" by Frederick J. Forster; "The Long Trail" by Monica Mayper; "The First Thanksgiving" by Barbara Juster Esbensen; "The Sounding Fog" by Susan Nichols Pulsifer; "In Cranberry Bog" by Nancy Dingman Watson; "Spring" by Marjorie Frost Fraser; "Summer" by Carolyn Hall; "Autumn" by Mary O'Neill; and "Winter" by Marchette Chute.

Discussion Starters and Multidisciplinary Activities

1. Ask students if, after reading the book, New England seems familiar or strange compared to where they live. Discuss this.

2. Have students share which of the book's poems is their favorite, and why.

3. Ask students to study the picture of cranberries in North Falmouth, Massachusetts, and discuss it. What has the artist done to make this picture special? How does the picture accentuate some of the lines of poetry from "In Cranberry Bog"?

4. Invite students to write poems about one or more seasons of the year. Gather these poems together and compile a classroom anthology titled "Book of Seasons." Have interested students illustrate the cover and interior of the book.

5. A poem of particular interest to readers learning about the early history of our country is "The Sea." This poem by an unknown author is a humorous account of the shore as being "a place where little fishes learn to swim and where clumsy sailors tumble in." Invite interested students to write a short story or poem featuring the shore from the point of view of a Pilgrim boy or girl.

6. There are many recipes for cranberry bread. Invite a few interested students to make loaves of cranberry bread at home, with help from parents, and to share the bread with the class, so everyone can have a taste.

The 1600s

Nonfiction Connections

- 📖 *Colonial American Craftspeople*
- 📖 *Colonial American Medicine*
- 📖 *Eating the Plates*
- 📖 *Growing Up in Colonial America*
- 📖 *Indians of the Northeast Woodlands*
- 📖 *Making Thirteen Colonies*
- 📖 *The Mayflower People: Triumphs and Tragedies*
- 📖 *Old Silver Leg Takes Over! A Story of Peter Stuyvesant*
- 📖 *Stranded at Plimoth Plantation, 1626*
- 📖 *Tapenum's Day: A Wampanoag Indian Boy in Pilgrim Times*
- 📖 *Thunder from the Clear Sky*

 *Colonial American Craftspeople*

by Bernardine S. Stevens
New York: Franklin Watts, 1993. 128p.

This book will appeal to readers in grades three through five. The illustrations are black-and-white reproductions.

This book guides the reader in exploring the crafts developed in the early years of our country, showing and describing the tools and techniques of coopers, joiners, and other woodworkers; masons, sawyers, bricklayers, and other builders; metalworkers, including silversmiths, blacksmiths, and farriers; leatherworkers; and papermakers, printers, and bookbinders.

The book begins with a section devoted to discussion of apprentices, craftspeople in training. Because many of the people who wanted to come to the American colonies did not have enough money to pay for their passage, they signed "indentures." These in- dentured servants sometimes worked for artisans and were called apprentices. Children as well as adults worked as indentured servants. The master taught the craft to the apprentice and provided food, clothing, and a place to sleep.

Because professional craftspeople were rare in the South, plantation owners often hired master builders. As free time increased, papermakers, printers, and bookbinders were needed to provide books and newspapers, as well as paper for conducting business. Goldsmiths and silversmiths made jewelry, clocks, and silver plate. Farriers shod horses and oxen. Cutlers shaped iron and steel into weapons and instruments. Other craftspeople made hats, wigs, and dresses in the newest fashions.

Possible Topics for Further Investigation

1 Arrange a convenient time for a group of interested students to visit a local woodworker's shop. Ask the woodworker to explain the work, demonstrate the various tools used, and show students finished pieces. Have students take notes and ask questions. Have the group share what they learn and send a thank you letter to the woodworker.

2 Students will enjoy making a sheet of paper: Fill a 1-cup measuring cup with toilet tissue torn into tiny pieces. Pour the tissue into a plastic bowl and add 4 cups of warm tap water. Reach into the liquid and tear the paper into smaller bits, until the "pulp" has the consistency of lumpy oatmeal. In the bottom of a baking pan, lay a piece of window screening (use a piece large enough to cover the sides and edges of the pan). Pour the pulp onto the screen. Lift out the screen, holding it level, and let it drain. Place the screen, pulpside up, on newspaper. Put two layers of newspaper on top of the pulp and use a rolling pin to squeeze out the water. Remove the newspapers, turn the screen over, and remove the screen. Allow the sheet of paper to dry.

3 Have students try potato printing: Cut potatoes in half and draw a design on the cut surfaces (e.g., a sun, moon, or star). Have an adult supervisor help students cut away the potato surrounding the design (the design should stand at least one-quarter inch above the surrounding surface). Moisten sponge and dip it into tempera paint. Press the potato stamp into the sponge and then use the stamp to print designs on paper.

📖 *Colonial American Medicine*

by Susan Neiburg Terkel

New York: Franklin Watts, 1993. 112p.

This book will appeal to third- through fifth-grade readers. The illustrations are black-and-white sketches.

Chapter 1 is a case history of the illness that eventually led to the death of George Washington. The patient was treated with bloodletting, purging, and blistering before he slipped into a coma and died. Many thought it was better to do nothing than to call on a colonial physician.

Chapter 2 describes the various illnesses that afflicted Pilgrims on their journey to the New World and during the first winter, and the diseases brought by Europeans to Native Americans. Chapter 3 discusses the various epidemics that struck the colonies.

Chapter 4 explains that most medical students in the colonies had not performed dissections or examined skeletons. Chapter 5, "A Sorry State of Affairs," points out that colonial doctors did not have clinical thermometers, X-rays, stethoscopes, or even watches with second hands to assist in diagnosis. Chapter 6 discusses the various recipes for medicines, and Chapter 7 explains that the healers had no formal medical training.

Chapter 8 examines the state of colonial hospitals and clinics, and Chapter 9 discusses casualties of war. Chapter 10 explains how colonists gradually learned to stay healthy by improving their diets and sanitation, and by taking inoculations.

Possible Topics for Further Investigation

1 Most school districts require all students (except those excused for religious reasons) to show proof of a medical examination and inoculations before enrolling them in school. Have a pair of students ask a school secretary what is required for medical clearance to attend school. Is there a standard form to document this? Do local doctors complete a "School Physical Report" or similar form? Have the students obtain copies of these forms and share and discuss them with the class.

2 Benjamin Franklin conducted many scientific experiments, including some that involved electricity. Have students make an "electroscope" to detect electricity: Cut a 1-by-4-inch strip of corrugated cardboard. Bend a paper clip into the shape of a fishhook. Push the straight part of the paper clip through the center of the cardboard strip. Cut a ¼-by-4-inch ribbon of aluminum foil and hang it from the hook. Rub a balloon and a comb with a piece of wool, each for 60 seconds. Hold the electroscope by the cardboard and bring it near the comb and the balloon. What happens to the foil?

3 Many people still recommend chicken soup as a remedy for the common cold. Ask interested students to write humorous poems or stories in which chicken soup is promoted as a cure for illness. As an example, read all or part of Maurice Sendak's humorous picture book *Chicken Soup with Rice* (New York: Harper & Row, 1962). Post the poems and stories on a classroom bulletin board.

From *Exploring Our Country's History.* © 1998 Phyllis J. Perry. Teacher Ideas Press. (800) 237-6124.

📖 *Eating the Plates*

by Lucille Recht Penner
New York: Macmillan, 1991. 118p.

This book about the eating habits, customs, and manners of the early Pilgrims will appeal to second- through fourth-grade readers. It is illustrated with black-and-white drawings and pictures taken from various historical archives.

One of the first foods the Pilgrims ate in the New World was mussels. These made everyone sick, so the Pilgrims ate the hard biscuits and salt beef they had brought with them. They found corn to plant the next spring; caught fish, lobsters, and crabs; hunted birds and animals; and found nuts and berries.

In the years that followed, the Pilgrims learned to build homes and survive in the new land. New settlers brought pigs, sheep, chickens, goats, and cows. They evaporated ocean water to obtain salt; they had milk and eggs; they baked bread, made cider, and grew vegetables. Cooking was often an all-day process in the big stone fireplaces that ranged from eight to ten feet in width. A lug pole, made of green wood, was stretched across the fireplace to support pots and kettles.

Food was brought to the table on chargers. No one had his or her own plate; they shared trenchers. Some used stale bread as a plate, ate the food on top, and then ate the plate. Spoons were often clamshells attached to sticks, and few people had forks. Cups were made of gourds or wood. Oftentimes, children stood around the table at mealtime because there were few chairs.

Possible Topics for Further Investigation

1 The last section of the book provides a menu. With adult help and supervision, have students plan a classroom Pilgrim feast. A committee might be charged with determining what foods will be served, taking into account available cooking facilities, cost, and the number of students available to prepare each item. A meal of four foods, with a committee of six students involved in preparing each food, is suggested (e.g., one committee might make fresh corn soup, another succotash stew, a third baked pumpkin stuffed with apple, and a fourth bannock cakes). Based on the number of people who will attend the feast, students should convert recipe quantities to make enough food. Have the committees make a master shopping list and organize the purchase or donation of supplies.

On the day of the feast, have adult volunteers and student committees prepare the foods. Hot plates or ovens should be available, as well as pots, pans, and other necessary utensils. Even with adult supervision, safety should be stressed and cleanliness emphasized.

2 Have students plan and do artistic touches for the feast: Each student might make a place mat depicting a Pilgrim scene or a table centerpiece. After the feast, the recipes selected might be printed and sent home with the students.

3 Class members should have the responsibility for writing thank you notes to all the adults who assisted with the Pilgrim feast in any way.

📖 *Growing Up in*
Colonial America

by Tracy Barrett
Brookfield, CT: Millbrook Press, 1995. 96p.

This book will appeal to students in grades three through five. Its illustrations are reproductions of photographs and drawings from several library archives. Although the book is included in this section, "The 1600s," much of the text also applies to the history of the 1700s.

The first section discusses how life in the colonies differed from colony to colony. For example, in Plymouth, the settlers built small houses with kitchen gardens. Church activities were a central part of life, and children often went to Dame Schools. In contrast, in the Chesapeake area, houses were often built in the middle of tobacco fields for easy access to crops. There were fewer women and children in this part of the country and far more blacks than in the northern areas.

Throughout the colonies, babies were raised in traditional ways. Both boys and girls were dressed in long robes. They often slept in cradles near the fireplace. Most people made their own clothes. Children often helped with tending flax in the fields and with spinning flax and wool. Dyes came from nutshells, bark, and berries. Girls were taught a variety of stitches and sometimes made a sampler. Patchwork quilts were made from scraps of old clothes.

Children also helped with household chores, such as making soap and candles and churning butter. As soon as they were old enough, they learned to hunt and fish. They dug for clams and oysters, and they worked in the fields planting and harvesting pumpkins, squash, and corn.

Possible Topics for Further Investigation

1   There is a description of "Good Fritters" on page 41 of the book. If a school kitchen is available, have a group of students, working with an adult, make apple fritters to serve to the class. If a school kitchen is not available, invite parent volunteers to take a group of students (after written permission slips are secured) to a nearby home to do the cooking. Students should first collect recipes, share them, choose one, and then convert recipe quantities to prepare enough fritters for the class.

2   Excellent material for math problems appears throughout the book. For example, have students reread the information on page 68 and work in pairs to prepare a simple bar graph to convey the information about parent mortality in the colonial families. Students could write children's ages along the horizontal axis and percentages of children per colony who had lost one or both parents along the vertical axis.

3   Divide the class into two groups. Have one group make a chart summarizing life in the Plymouth colony, while the other group makes a chart summarizing life in the Chesapeake colonies. The same headings should be used along the left side of each chart, such as "Types of Homes," "Religion," "Making a Living," "Education," "Beliefs About Raising Children," and so on. To the right of these headings, groups should note appropriate information. For example, under "Beliefs About Raising Children" for the Plymouth chart, students might note that the Puritans thought children were born sinful. Post both charts on a classroom bulletin board and discuss the similarities and differences between life in the Plymouth colony and life in the Chesapeake colonies.

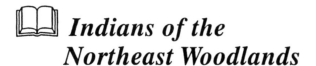 *Indians of the Northeast Woodlands*

NONFICTION
CONNECTIONS

by Beatrice Siegel
illustrated by William Sauts Bock
New York: Walker, 1992. 96p.

This book with black-and-white illustrations is appropriate for readers in grades three through five.

The book opens by discussing the tens of thousands of Algonquian who lived in the northeast woodlands. They were divided into large and small tribes, but all were part of the Algonquian family and spoke a variation of the Algonquian language. Each tribe was an independent nation with leaders and territory.

The Algonquian ate game that they hunted, such as deer, moose, rabbit, duck, turkey, and partridge. They also planted maize, beans, squash, and pumpkins, and gathered fruits and berries. They used bows and arrows and implements made of wood, shells, bone, and stone. They fished with nets, spears, and hooks. Sometimes, to signify particular ceremonies and events, they painted their faces and bodies with colored pigments.

Their summer villages were clusters of wigwams, which were easy to assemble, dismantle, and move. In winter, they lived in longhouses. They traveled by foot and canoe. Children learned by listening to, watching, and copying their elders. The Algonquian had faith in one Creator.

Wars between the Algonquian and the white settlers lasted many years. Eventually, the Algonquian lost their land to the settlers. In 1990, 37,000 Native Americans still lived in the northeast states in cities and on reservations.

Possible Topics for Further Investigation

1 White settlers drove Native Americans off their land. In recent years, Native Americans have assimilated into the general culture or have continued to live on reservations. Often, when the rights of Native Americans are violated, they take issues of concern to the courts. The Native American Rights Fund in Colorado is one group that continues to fight for the recognition of their rights. Invite a pair of students to write to this group at 1506 Broadway, Boulder, CO 80302, requesting available information about their work. The students should include a 9-by-12-inch self-addressed, stamped manila envelope. Have students share with the class any materials they receive.

2 Many Native American myths and legends have been published in picture-book format. Have a group of students, with help from a library media specialist, explore Native American mythology and folklore. The students should choose a favorite myth or legend and share it with the class orally, as a play, or as a puppet show.

3 Depending on where you live, there may be an interesting site to visit that houses Native American artifacts such as pottery, quill work, and baskets. It may be a section of a museum or an exhibit devoted entirely to Native American arts. Many such sites (in New England) are mentioned in Chapter 15 of the book, but there are many sites in other sections of the country, as well as traveling exhibits, which may be coming to your area soon. If possible, arrange for a class visit.

📖 *Making Thirteen Colonies*

by Joy Hakim
New York: Oxford University Press, 1993. 160p.

NONFICTION CONNECTIONS

This book will appeal to readers in grades four and five. With black-and-white illustrations, the book is divided into 42 chapters.

The first chapters describe the early 1600s, when Europe faced religious and economic problems, and faraway America seemed like a Garden of Eden. Ships landed in Chesapeake Bay, Virginia, in 1607. It was the first English colony to survive in the New World, but the settlers almost starved that first year. The following year, under the leadership of Lord de la Ware, conditions improved and more settlers came.

Beginning with Chapter 13, the reader learns about the *Mayflower* and the Saints and Strangers who settled in Plymouth, Massachusetts. These settlers faced many hardships. Roger Williams was too tolerant for the Puritans, so he was banished and began a new colony in Providence, Rhode Island.

Chapter 21 explains the beginnings of Connecticut, New Hampshire, and Maine. Chapter 25 discusses Peter Stuyvesant and his activities in New York. Chapter 26 describes the beginnings of New Jersey. Chapter 28 gives an account of William Penn and the beginnings of Pennsylvania. Chapter 30 discusses George Calvert's involvement in the beginnings of Maryland. Chapter 35 chronicles the development of North and South Carolina. Chapter 39 completes the presentation of the original 13 colonies with a discussion of Georgia.

Possible Topics for Further Investigation

1 Anne Hutchinson was the mother of 14 children, yet she found time to question the ministers among the Puritans in Massachusetts and to share her ideas about God. She was put on trial, exiled from the state, and went to Rhode Island. Have a group of students, with help from a library media specialist, research Anne Hutchinson. They might present what they learn as questions and answers in the form of a mock trial.

2 Divide the class into eight groups of two to four members per group. Have each group research a particular section of the chronology listed on page 154 of the book. Appropriate divisions for the eight groups might be: 1607–14, 1619–26, 1630–40, 1649–64, 1665–80, 1681–92, 1699–1732, and 1734–75. Ask each group to choose an event or an historical person from the time period. Have each group write a brief report about the event or person, and draw or photocopy (if copyright allows) an appropriate picture. Display the reports in the classroom as a timeline.

3 In 1953 Arthur Miller published his play *The Crucible*, about the Salem witch trials. Have an interested group of students read and discuss this play, choosing one section to present to the class as a reader's theatre, during which students read from scripts. Or, students might memorize parts of the play and present them to the class. In either case, students might want to wear simple costumes for dramatic effect.

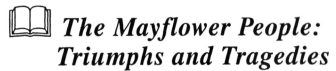 **The Mayflower People: Triumphs and Tragedies**

NONFICTION CONNECTIONS

by Anna W. Hale

Tucson, AZ: Harbinger House, 1995. 93p.

This book is appropriate for readers in grades three through five. It concerns real people and real events as described in letters and other historical documents, but dialogue has been added. A few black-and-white illustrations are included.

The book is divided into five chapters. Chapter 1 begins with the sailing of the *Speedwell* and the *Mayflower* in Southampton, England, in 1620. After five days, the ships turn back because the *Speedwell* is leaking. Again they sail, and again the *Speedwell* signals distress. Both ships turn back and return to Plymouth, England. On September 5, the *Mayflower* sails again, finally dropping anchor at Cape Cod on November 10.

Chapter 2 describes the Mayflower Compact and the problems associated with having landed not in Virginia but in Massachusetts. Chapter 3 details the story of Squanto, a Native American who is kidnapped as a boy from his Wampanoag village in Patuxet and taken to London. Squanto returns to find that his people have died of a plague and goes to live with the Wampanoags. He was there when the Pilgrims landed.

Chapter 4 describes the shocks and surprises that the Pilgrims face during their first winter. In the spring, Squanto helps them plant new crops. Chapter 5 is an account of the first Thanksgiving and the arrival of the good ship *Fortunate*, bearing supplies, family members, and friends. The book concludes with the author's notes, a glossary, and a list, by family groups, of everyone who sailed aboard the *Mayflower*.

Possible Topics for Further Investigation

1 Squanto was kidnapped and taken to London. He desperately wanted to return to his native village. Before he returned, he went to a monastery in Spain, to Nova Scotia, back to England, and finally returned to Massachusetts. Have a pair of interested students make a map showing the dates and places of Squanto's travels. Hang the map on a classroom bulletin board.

2 The Pilgrims were lucky to find corn, which they saved to plant in the spring. Have students conduct an experiment with corn: Fill a glass jar to the brim with dry corn kernels. Slowly pour in water, filling the jar to the brim. Set a small plastic plate on top of the jar. The next morning, check the jar. What has happened? Did the corn swell sufficiently with water to push the plate off the jar?

3 Pilgrims included many foods with corn in their diet. Have students, working with adult volunteers, make cornbread to share with the class. First, preheat an oven to 425°F and grease an 8-by-8-by-2-inch baking pan with shortening. Melt ¼ cup of shortening in a saucepan over low heat. Put 1 cup cornmeal, 1 cup flour, 1 tablespoon baking powder, 1 teaspoon sugar, and ¼ teaspoon salt in a mixing bowl. Mix well and add the melted shortening. Add 1 egg and 1 cup milk. Stir to blend. Pour the mixture into the baking pan and bake for 20 minutes. An adult should take the pan out of the oven and cut the cornbread into small squares.

 ## *Old Silver Leg Takes Over! A Story of Peter Stuyvesant*

NONFICTION CONNECTIONS

by Robert Quackenbush
Englewood Cliffs, NJ: Prentice-Hall, 1986. 36p.

This book will appeal to students in kindergarten through third grade. It is illustrated with humorous drawings. Scattered throughout the book are cartoon-like drawings of pigs making comments.

The book begins by describing the youth of Peter Stuyvesant, who was born in Holland in 1592. As soon as he finishes school, he goes to work for the Dutch East India Company. Shortly thereafter, he is appointed governor of Curacao, where he stays for 18 months. During a battle on the island of Saint Martin, Stuyvesant is hit in the right leg by a cannonball. He is fitted with a wooden leg decorated with silver.

Peter marries and is offered the job of governor of New Amsterdam by the Dutch West India Company. He arrives in New Amsterdam with his wife in 1647 to find a miserable community. He strives to bring order by requiring taverns to close earlier and by fining people for brawling and drinking on Sunday. He has pens built for pigs, has chimneys cleaned, and collects a tax to repair the fort.

People want more control of their government, so in addition to having Stuyvesant as the director general, the Dutch West India Company adds a council. They pass laws and govern successfully.

War erupts between Holland and England. In 1664, New Netherlands surrenders to the English, and New Amsterdam becomes New York. Stuyvesant goes to Holland, is pardoned by his company, and returns to New Amsterdam to live a quiet life with his family.

Possible Topics for Further Investigation

1 Peter Stuyvesant was a colorful character whose sister had a good deal of influence over him. When Stuyvesant was angry, he would stomp his peg leg. Have students write original poems about Peter Stuyvesant. They may be serious or humorous, and should mention his silver leg. Display the poems in the classroom.

2 The government of New Amsterdam consisted of Peter Stuyvesant as director general, two burgomasters (mayors), five schepens (heads of districts), and a schout (sheriff). Have students discuss the governing body of your town, city, or county. Invite students to study the structure of the local government and draw a chart showing its organization, including the names of the individuals who currently hold office. Display the chart in the classroom.

3 Invite a member of the local government to visit the class and explain how decisions and laws are made and executed. Ask students to write out questions ahead of time and submit these questions to the guest speaker prior to the class visit. After the visit, have students send a thank you letter to the guest.

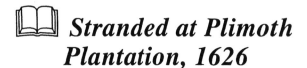 *Stranded at Plimoth Plantation, 1626*

NONFICTION CONNECTIONS

by Gary Bowen
New York: HarperCollins, 1994. 81p.

This is a large-format book with many illustrations by the author. The illustrations are reproductions of woodcuts that were cut on cherry and pearwood, printed, and hand-colored with inks. The story is told in the form of diary entries and will appeal to students in grades two through five.

The story begins with an entry dated November 22, 1626. The narrator, Christopher Sears, is an indentured servant to Captain Sibsey on the *Sparrowhawk*, sailing for Jamestown, Virginia. They shipwreck on the New England shore, finding themselves stranded and without shelter. In the wreck, Christopher injures his leg.

Native Americans bring help from Plimoth Plantation. All are transported to Plimoth to remain until a ship can take them 700 miles south to Jamestown. Christopher goes to live with the Brewster family and makes woodcuts to print in his diary while he rests and his leg heals.

The entries that follow detail life on the plantation, including court day, Sabbath day, watching the militia drill, learning to play the drums, tutoring, cutting lumber, trading with the Native Americans, catching eels, fishing and mending nets, taking a bath, the birth of a baby, attending a funeral, going to street dances, mending fences, working plots of land, spotting an eagle, attending a wedding, and watching the aurora borealis.

When Christopher turns 14, he is allowed to choose his guardian. He decides to remain at Plimoth Plantation.

Possible Topics for Further Investigation

1. Windows in the homes at Plimoth Plantation were made of oiled paper, the paper being matted sheets of cellulose fibers. Oil filled the air spaces among the fibers, making the paper opaque but not translucent. Have students rub a spot of oil on a sheet of paper and hold the sheet about 12 inches in front of a bright lamp. Because the spaces among the fibers are filled with oil, the composition of this portion of the paper becomes more uniform, allowing more light to pass through it.

2. Enlist the aid of an art specialist in sharing woodcuts with the class and helping students make prints. If woodcuts are too difficult, the art specialist might show students how to make potato stamps (cut a potato in half, draw a design on the cut surface, and cut away the potato surrounding the design). Students might try seasonal designs (e.g., simple flowers, hearts, shamrocks, etc.) and print cards.

3. Breadmaking is often mentioned in the diary entries. Christopher explains that the people of Plimoth Plantation grind coarse meal by hand. "One-Third Bread" has equal parts wheat, rye, and corn flours. Have interested students find an old New England bread recipe and, with adult supervision, make the dough and bake two loaves of bread for the class, either at school or at home. Have the students share the recipe and its origin. Have butter and jelly available for the tasting.

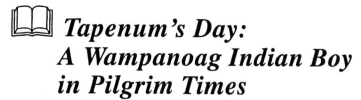

Tapenum's Day: A Wampanoag Indian Boy in Pilgrim Times

NONFICTION CONNECTIONS

by Kate Waters
photographs by Russ Kendall
New York: Scholastic, 1996. 40p.

This book will appeal to second-through fourth-grade readers. It is part of a trilogy of books describing the life of children living in Massachusetts in the 1620s. The book is filled with color photographs.

This book explores the life of a Wampanoag boy in the 1620s through photographs of Isaac Hendricks, a modern-day Native American boy who was 11 when the photographs were taken. In the photographs, the book makes use of the Wampanoag Indian Program at Plimoth Plantation. This program has a homesite at Plimoth Plantation called Hobbamock's Homesite. Modern-day visitors can see how members of a Wampanoag family planted and tended corn, wove mats and baskets, and prepared food.

Isaac plays the role of Tapenum, who wants to be selected to be a warrior. When he is not selected for this honor, Tapenum enacts a plan to increase his strength and improve his tracking skills so that he might be chosen for this honor another year.

Tapenum goes hunting with his bow and arrow. He runs a great distance to increase his strength. Tapenum meets an old Wampanoag named Waban, who shows him how to prepare sinew and glue to make a high-quality arrow. The last part of the book contains maps, explains Wampanoag words, and provides information about the Wampanoag Indian Program.

Possible Topics for Further Investigation

1 Students studying a variety of books on the topic of the early settlers in America will benefit from a good map of the area. Using the map on page 37 of the book, invite a small group of students to prepare a large wall map of the area depicted, to be displayed in the classroom. The map should show Massachusetts, part of Rhode Island, and some of the larger coastal islands. Have the students include the place names, as they were known in the 1600s and as they are known today.

2 The Wampanoag name for oak is *nootimis* (NOO-ta-miss); the name for wind is *waban* (WAY-ban). Invite a pair of interested students to write an original legend about the oak and the wind. Have the students use word processing software to print the final text, allowing space on each page for illustrations. Have the students illustrate their legend and share it with the class (or with another class in the school).

3 Have students make shoebox dioramas of a 1620s Wampanoag village, consulting photographs in the book. To make a small *wetu*, or "house," the students might try weaving grasses and thin sticks to make a structure that resembles the one shown on page 5 of the book. Other students might want to depict a farming, fishing, or hunting scene. Some might depict a family scene using cut-out figures dressed in appropriate clothing and jewelry. Have students share their dioramas and describe the scene.

From *Exploring Our Country's History*. © 1998 Phyllis J. Perry. Teacher Ideas Press. (800) 237-6124.

 **Thunder from the Clear Sky**

NONFICTION
CONNECTIONS

written and illustrated by Marcia Sewall
New York: Atheneum Books for Young Readers, 1995. 56p.

This picture book should be read with teacher guidance. The simple and colorful illustrations depict violent as well as peaceful scenes. It is appropriate for third- and fourth-grade readers.

The book begins with a Wampanoag story about settlers arriving in the New World. For the most part, relations are peaceful. The Wampanoag trade with the white settlers, exchanging furs and corn for trinkets, cloth, and metal tools.

Distrust grows when the whites kidnap several Wampanoag and sail away with them. The Wampanoag suffer from diseases introduced by the white settlers. Chief Massasoit is involved in the drafting of a peace treaty, but some of the trading provisions are not favorable to the Wampanoag. More settlers come, slowly forcing the Wampanoag from their lands. They remain at peace with the settlers, but natives of the Massachusetts nation living nearby are attacked. After Massasoit's death, this peaceful period ends.

The second story in the book is told by an old Pilgrim, who describes the early settlement in Cape Cod. In 1675, he sees the settlers and Native Americans killing each other.

The book then alternates points of view, Native American and Pilgrim, as war erupts. Native Americans and whites are killed. Some Native Americans are taken as slaves. Many tribes are involved. Sometimes, a Native American betrays other Native Americans. An old Native American prophecy that whites would come from across the sea and force them from their lands has become reality.

Possible Topics for Further Investigation

1 On page 5 of the book is a story in which the Native Americans, upon first seeing a large sailing boat, mistake it for an island covered in trees hung with white clouds. Hold a brief class brainstorming session to list other items brought by the Europeans that Native Americans had never seen. Invite students to select an item from the list and write a short story from the Native American viewpoint describing the first sighting of the item and "explaining" the event.

2 Beaver were important to the North American fur trade. Invite a pair of students to research beaver fur, including its uses and its arrival in England and Europe. Have the students draw or photocopy (if copyright allows) pictures of products that made use of beaver fur. Have the students share with the class what they learn.

3 Have students assign roles, write dialogue, and hold a mock trial in the classroom inquiring into the death of John Sassamon. King Philip and other warriors claimed that the victim died accidentally. Patuckson said that he witnessed the event and knew that it was murder. Tobias, his son, and another warrior were accused of the crime. Class members who do not have roles should serve as a jury. After all the witnesses are called and have a chance to testify, the jury should meet and render a verdict.

Part II
The 1700s

The 1700s

● FICTION ●

📖 *The Boston Coffee Party*
📖 *Changes for Felicity*
📖 *An Enemy Among Them*
📖 *George Washington's Socks*
📖 *Guns for General Washington: A Story of the American Revolution*

📖 *The Hessian's Secret Diary*
📖 *Katie's Trunk*
📖 *A Ride into Morning*
📖 *Samuel's Choice*
📖 *A Spy in the King's Colony*
📖 *Time Enough for Drums*

◆ BRIDGES AND POETRY ◆

📖 *Doodle Dandy! The Complete Book of Independence Day Words*
📖 *The Winter of Red Snow*
📖 *Year-Round Programs for Young Players*

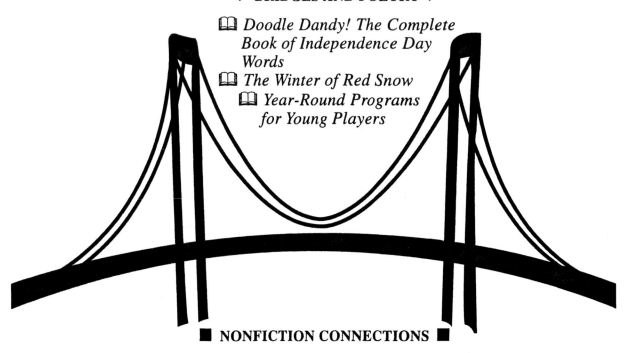

■ NONFICTION CONNECTIONS ■

📖 *The American Revolution: How We Fought the War of Independence*
📖 *The Ben Franklin Book of Easy and Incredible Experiments*
📖 *Book of the New American Nation*
📖 *The Boston Tea Party*
📖 *The Fall of Quebec and the French and Indian War*
📖 *If You Were There in 1776*

📖 *A Multicultural Portrait of the American Revolution*
📖 *Paul Revere*
📖 *A Picture Book of George Washington*
📖 *The Revolutionary War: A Sourcebook on Colonial America*
📖 *A Young Patriot: The American Revolution As Experienced by One Boy*

—OTHER TOPICS TO EXPLORE—

—Abigail Adams	—General Howe	—Quebec Act	—Thomas Paine
—Bunker Hill	—Loyalists	—Stamp Act	—Townshend Acts
—Declaratory Act	—Molly Pitcher	—Sugar Act	—Treaty of Paris

From *Exploring Our Country's History*. © 1998 Phyllis J. Perry. Teacher Ideas Press. (800) 237-6124.

● *Fiction* ●

- 📖 *The Boston Coffee Party*
- 📖 *Changes for Felicity*
- 📖 *An Enemy Among Them*
- 📖 *George Washington's Socks*
- 📖 *Guns for General Washington: A Story of the American Revolution*
- 📖 *The Hessian's Secret Diary*
- 📖 *Katie's Trunk*
- 📖 *A Ride into Morning*
- 📖 *Samuel's Choice*
- 📖 *A Spy in the King's Colony*
- 📖 *Time Enough for Drums*

The Boston Coffee Party

FICTION

by Doreen Rappaport
illustrated by Emily Arnold McCully
New York: Harper & Row, 1988. 64p.

This book, part of the I Can Read series, will appeal to students in kindergarten through third grade. Color illustrations complement the text.

As the story begins, Emma and her sister, Sarah, are sent by their mother, Mrs. Homans, to the store for sugar. First, they go to Merchant Smith's shop, but they find no sugar, which is scarce because of the war. The children go from shop to shop, but it's always the same: No sugar.

Finally, the girls go to Merchant Thomas's shop. Although everyone else is charging 5 shillings per pound, Merchant Thomas is charging 7 shillings per pound. He has a few pounds of sugar left. Sarah puts her money on the counter. Just then,

Mrs. Arnold walks into the store, asking for sugar. Merchant Thomas immediately sells the last of the sugar to her for 8 shillings per pound. He ignores the girls' comments.

The next chapter describes a sewing party. Mrs. Homans tells the group that Merchant Thomas is charging too much for sugar. Aunt Harriet joins them and says that Merchant Thomas has locked 40 barrels of coffee in his warehouse and is waiting to sell it for a high price when no one else in Boston has coffee.

In the final chapter, the women and children bring pots to Merchant Thomas's shop. They steal the keys to the warehouse, empty the coffee into their pots, and take it home.

Discussion Starters and Multidisciplinary Activities

1 Have students discuss what happened when Mrs. Arnold entered Merchant Thomas's shop. Was it fair for the merchant to sell the sugar to someone else when he had quoted a price to the girls and they had put their money on the counter?

2 When the women took the keys from Merchant Thomas and took all his coffee, they were stealing. Discuss this with students. Were the women wrong to take the merchant's coffee? Why?

3 The women threaten Merchant Thomas, saying that he will be sorry when their men return from the war. Have students discuss what they think might happen after the war, when the men return and learn how Merchant Thomas has behaved.

4 Merchant Thomas charged 8 shillings per pound for sugar. Have students research how much sugar costs per pound today. How much is an English shilling worth today in American money? How many shillings per pound would sugar cost today?

5 Sarah suggests holding a party like the men held when they "threw English tea into the harbor." Invite a small group of students to research the Boston Tea Party and share with the class what they learn.

6 Have a group of students dramatize this story. Have boys play the roles of the merchants who have no coffee and the role of Merchant Thomas. Girls should play the roles of Emma, Sarah, Mrs. Homans, and Aunt Harriet. Props should include cloth, needles, thread, boxes (for barrels), pots, and a wagon. Have the actors present their play to the class.

 *Changes for Felicity*

by Valerie Tripp
Middleton, WI: Pleasant, 1992. 69p.

FICTION

This book will appeal to second- and third-grade readers. The central character, Felicity Merriman, is a colonial girl growing up just before the American Revolution. Color illustrations complement the text.

As the story begins, Felicity is playing with dolls with her friend Elizabeth. Felicity's grandfather comes and points out that he and Elizabeth's family are among the last of the Loyalists. They go to the stable to see Felicity's horse, Penny. Grandfather explains that Penny will have a foal this spring.

Felicity and Elizabeth offer to take currycombs to Mr. Pelham, the town jailer. At the jail, they see a very sick man, Mr. Nye. Because Mr. Nye had tried to steal Felicity's horse, she has no sympathy for him, but Elizabeth persuades Felicity to join her the next day in bringing blankets and medicine for the man.

The next day, Felicity learns that Elizabeth's father has been jailed because he is a Loyalist. Grandfather goes out in the rain to try to help. The next day, Grandfather is gravely ill; a few days later, he dies. Felicity's mother gives her a chest containing a green riding habit that Grandfather had planned to give her on her birthday.

Although Grandfather got Elizabeth's father released from jail, her father must go to New York to be safe. At the jail, the girls learn that Mr. Nye is well and has been released. When Penny experiences trouble giving birth, Mr. Nye comes to help deliver the foal, which they name Patriot.

Discussion Starters and Multidisciplinary Activities

1 Have students discuss their reactions to the scene in which the girls see Mr. Nye so ill in jail. Did they think Felicity would immediately feel sorry for him? Did they think that Elizabeth would change Felicity's mind? Did they guess that Mr. Nye would in some way repay Felicity's favor?

2 The sampler plays a major role in the book. Have students discuss the message on the sampler and its meaning in this story.

3 Although the beginning and the ending of this story are similar, the girls have changed during the course of the story. Have students discuss these changes.

4 A snake with the slogan "join or die" appears on pages 64 and 65 of the book. Have students make posters with symbols and slogans that might have been used to convince citizens in various parts of the colonies to join the Patriots. Display the posters in the classroom.

5 Stitchery, embroidery, and making samplers are no longer common activities. Invite to class someone from the community who does stitchery. Ask the guest to bring a sampler and demonstrate the process of making one. After the visit, have students send a thank you letter to the guest.

6 Jails have changed since the time period depicted in the book. Invite a small group of students to research a nearby jail. Who is in charge of the jail? How many prisoners does it hold? How are the costs of maintaining a jail paid? In an oral presentation, have the students share with the class what they learn.

📖 *An Enemy Among Them*

FICTION

by Deborah H. DeFord and Harry S. Stout
Boston: Houghton Mifflin, 1987. 203p.

This book will appeal to fourth- and fifth-grade readers. The story takes place in 1776.

One part of the story traces the experiences of a Hessian soldier, Christian, while another part follows the experiences of Margaret Volpert, whose family lives on a farm in Pennsylvania. Margaret's brother, John, is a Patriot soldier. Her other brother, Jacob, is waiting for his 18th birthday so he can join the Patriots.

Jacob tells Margaret that her longtime friend George is not a Patriot. John is discharged, but when Jacob joins the army, John re-enlists. When the brothers and Christian are fighting on the same battlefield, John and Christian are both wounded. Margaret and her mother find John and Christian in the same hospital. They stay and nurse the soldiers as long as possible.

Mr. Volpert goes to the hospital, visits his son, and takes Christian with him to work in his shoe shop. George tries vainly to enlist Christian to spy for the British. A dying John teaches Christian about the importance of freedom.

After John dies, Christian confesses to Margaret that his bayonet killed John. Christian runs to the Patriots with information about how they can take the fort at Stony Point. George and Margaret chase after him. When they meet, Christian kills George to protect Margaret. Christian and Margaret find the Continental army, and Christian fights alongside Jacob to take the fort. Margaret waits at home for the war to end so that she can marry Christian.

Discussion Starters and Multidisciplinary Activities

1 Have students discuss why they think Mr. Volpert is more understanding of the Hessian soldiers than Mrs. Volpert.

2 Charlotte Volpert appears to be the least important of the Volpert children in this story, yet she plays an important role. Have students discuss Charlotte's role in the story.

3 Christian seems to believe that, by joining the Continental army and protecting Jacob, he can redeem himself for having killed John. Margaret and Jacob, and Christian himself, never tell John's parents that it was Christian's bayonet that killed John. Have students discuss whether it was wise to keep this secret.

4 A few German words are present in the story, giving the dialogue flavor. Invite two high school students who are studying German to visit the class and present a brief conversation in German. The high school students might teach the class a few words of German. After the visit, have students send thank you letters to the guests.

5 In Chapter 6, John and Christian discuss the rebel cause. Christian believes that the colonists should be loyal to their king and should be willing to pay taxes. John argues that there can't be taxation without representation. Invite two students to role-play this conversation between two men who fought on opposite sides on the battlefield.

6 Have a pair of students use a map with a scale in miles to determine how many miles Margaret traveled from Reading to Sandy Beach, including her return through Bethlehem, Changewater, Walpack, Sussex, and Stony Point. Do these cities still exit today?

📖 *George Washington's Socks*

FICTION

by Elvira Woodruff

New York: Scholastic, 1991. 166p.

Students in grades three through five will enjoy this historical fantasy about the American Revolution. It has no illustrations.

Four fifth-grade boys, Matt, Quentin, Hooter, and Tony, form an adventure club. At every meeting, they will read about one real, historical adventure. For the first camp-out adventure, Matt is maneuvered into taking with him his little sister, Katie, who brings along her squirt gun and other "weapons."

They gather at Tony's, and Matt begins to read about Washington crossing the Delaware. The situation is tame, so Matt suggests a night hike along Levy Lake, which is reputed to be haunted. When they reach the lake, an old rowboat appears. Under a spell, the children climb aboard. Suddenly, it is snowing, and their boat is in a thick ice floe.

Katie falls out of the boat. Another boat appears, and General Washington rescues Katie and then the boys, who realize that they have traveled back in time.

They cross the river, and Matt leaves the others to return General Washington's cloak. He joins up with other rebels and makes friends with a young man, who dies along the way. A farmer helps Matt and loans him a mule. Matt finds two of his friends but is told that Katie and Quentin have been taken by Hessians. Native Americans help the boys find Katie and Quentin, and a Hessian saves Katie from drowning. Rebels reappear and kill the Hessian. The children find the rowboat again and time-travel back to Levy Lake.

Discussion Starters and Multidisciplinary Activities

1 At first, Matt was afraid to climb onto Blackjack's back, but before long, he was talking to the mule and finally had tears in his eyes when he bid the mule farewell. Have students discuss what made this mule so special to Matt.

2 When the Hessian Gustav is killed, Hooter begins to cry. He says that it's not like television because in real life, you can't always tell the good guys from the bad guys. Have students discuss what it was that Hooter was describing.

3 The first sign of being in the present time was a potato chip bag. Have students discuss other clues that might have suggested the children were in the present time.

4 The name of the magical boat, Emit Levart, spelled backwards in the same word order is Time Travel. The children didn't realize this until they saw it reflected in the water. Have students write brief coded messages that can only be decoded when held up to a mirror.

5 The rebels appreciate wool socks and coats, and Matt is glad he wore his down vest. Today, when mountaineers climb to high elevations, where it will be wet and cold, they take special clothing, packs, sleeping bags, and tents. Have students discuss modern mountaineering equipment and materials. Have a small group of students investigate this topic by talking with someone in a local mountaineering shop, or by writing for a catalogue from a mountaineering company. Have the students share what they learn with the class.

6 Blackjack was a mule. Have a student write a brief report about mules. How are mules different from donkeys and horses?

Guns for General Washington: A Story of the American Revolution

FICTION

by Seymour Reit

San Diego, CA: Harcourt Brace Jovanovich, 1990. 98p.

This book will appeal to readers in grades three through five. The central character is young Will Knox.

In the winter of 1775, the British attack Boston Harbor. Washington's troops have little ammunition and no big cannons. Will Knox is only 19, but he is a soldier, along with his brother, Colonel Henry Knox. General Washington approves Colonel Knox's plan to travel 300 miles north to Fort Ticonderoga to obtain cannons and ammunition and bring them back to Cambridge.

Henry and Will leave camp and go to Albany, where General Schuyler helps them arrange for the building of carts and sleds. Henry and Will continue onward to Fort Ticonderoga, where they ask for volunteers to help take the guns and ammunition to General Washington. They load the guns and cross Lake George.

At Fort George, the overland trip begins. The carts and sleds are ready. A farmer and his young son join the team. Slowly, they move from Fort George to Glens Falls, and across the Mohawk River. They follow the trail of the west bank of the Hudson south of Albany to Westfield, Springfield, Worcester, and finally to Cambridge.

Secretly, the cannons are put in place on the Heights and fired upon the British ships. The British sail away, and this major Revolutionary effort succeeds.

Discussion Starters and Multidisciplinary Activities

1 Young Paul Revere does not make the dangerous journey with the cannons, yet he plays an important role in the story. Have students discuss Revere's role.

2 When everyone at the War Council argues against Henry's plan to bring the cannons overland, General Washington gives Henry permission to attempt this dangerous task. Have students discuss why General Washington was ready to take this risk.

3 Farmer Becker and his son, J. P., are brave members of Colonel Knox's crew. Have students discuss their contributions to bringing the guns to General Washington.

4 The author of the book, Seymour Reit, has written more than 80 books for young people, including *Behind Rebel Lines*. He also created "Casper the Friendly Ghost." Invite a group of students who particularly enjoyed *Guns for General Washington* to read other Reit books and present brief oral book reports to the class.

5 Have a small group of students, with help from a library media specialist, project a map of the northeastern United States onto chart paper or posterboard using an overhead projector. Have students trace the enlarged image and display the map in the classroom.

6 Have students locate the major locales mentioned in the story on the map created in activity 5. Use symbols to show General Washington at Cambridge, General Howe's ships in Boston Harbor, Fort Ticonderoga, and the major lakes, rivers, and towns. Display the map on a classroom bulletin board.

 *The Hessian's Secret Diary*

FICTION

by Lisa Banim
illustrated by James Watling
New York: Silver Moon Press, 1996. 74p.

This book will appeal to readers in grades two through four. It is illustrated with several black-and-white sketches.

The story takes place in Brooklyn, New York, centered around the van Brundt family's farm in 1776. Even though Redcoats are afoot, 10-year-old Peggy van Brundt slips out of the house whenever she can, to go with her dog, Patches, to enjoy the nearby woods and stream and to make sketches.

While out sketching one day, Peggy catches a glimpse of someone in a dirty uniform. On her next trip, Peggy catches sight of him, but again he disappears. She finds his sketchbook, which is filled with foreign words and beautiful sketches.

Peggy follows the path of the stranger to an old deserted barn. She manages to explain to the wounded man that she has his sketchbook, and leaves her sketchbook with him. She promises to return with food and a blanket. The Redcoats come to the van Brundt farm and search Peggy's home, finding the stranger's sketchbook. Peggy says that she found it in the woods, but Redcoats take it with them.

Peggy stays near home, worrying about her two brothers, who are fighting for the Americans. When Peggy returns to the barn, she finds that the stranger has left. Her sketchbook is there, with a new drawing in it. A Redcoat lieutenant returns the sketchbook Peggy found, telling her that it must have belonged to a Hessian deserter. As the story ends, Peggy wonders if she will ever again see the Hessian.

Discussion Starters and Multidisciplinary Activities

1 Being only 10 years old helps Peggy van Brundt in this story. Have students discuss how Peggy's youth and seeming innocence help her fool the Redcoats.

2 Peggy's parents try to be fair but firm with her. Have students point out passages in the text that support this statement.

3 Patches is a good companion, but he also causes a number of problems for Peggy. Have students point out passages in the text that support this statement.

4 Invite an interested group of students to keep a diary for one week, including sketches of various events that take place at school and at home. Allow students who wish to share their diaries and sketches with others in the class.

5 During the Revolution, the soldiers hired by King George III of England were called Hessians because the majority of them (about 8,000) came from two German principalities, Hesse-Cassel and Hesse-Hanau. Have a pair of students, working with a library media specialist or adult volunteer, research these principalities and locate them on a map. Have the students share their findings with the class.

6 Invite a pair of students to locate on a map of the United States the following places mentioned in the book: Manhattan Island, Gravesend Bay, Brooklyn, Gowanus and Bradford Pass, the East River, Welfare Island (now known as Roosevelt Island), White Plains, and Long Island. Have the students share their findings with the class.

From *Exploring Our Country's History.* © 1998 Phyllis J. Perry. Teacher Ideas Press. (800) 237-6124.

 ## *Katie's Trunk*

FICTION

by Ann Turner
illustrated by Ron Himler
New York: Macmillan, 1992. 32p. (unnumbered)

This book will appeal to students in kindergarten through third grade. Full-color illustrations complement the text.

As the story begins, Katie's mother tells her that she should sit down "to sew long seams all day and get the goodness straight inside." All Katie knows is that she feels uneasy, as if a storm is coming.

Because Katie and her family are Tories, some people in town no longer speak to them. Celia Warren no longer speaks to Katie. Celia's brother, Ralph, no longer speaks to Katie's brother, Walter. Katie knows that rebels are marching and conducting drills beyond the meadows.

One day, Katie's father comes rushing toward their home and tells her to get her mother and hide in the woods because the rebels are coming. The whole family hides. Katie crouches down with the others but finds that she can't wait idly. She races to her home to protect it.

Once inside, Katie touches all the things that she loves. When she hears angry voices, Katie hides beneath the dresses in her mother's trunk. John Warren comes into the room and lifts some dresses from the trunk. He touches Katie and then shouts, "The Tories are coming!" He leaves the trunk open as the rebels flee. Katie realizes that John Warren has left a seam of goodness there.

Discussion Starters and Multidisciplinary Activities

1 Katie "feels something" in the air. Have students discuss the sensations they have felt when worried or eagerly anticipating some event.

2 Instead of hiding quietly in the shrubbery, Katie breaks away and runs to the house, putting herself in danger. Have students discuss how each family member reacted when they returned to the house to find Katie there.

3 Have students discuss why they think John Warren did not mention that he'd found Katie, and why he led the rebels out of the house and onto the road.

4 Have a pair of students, with help from an adult volunteer, research this period of time. Why was Katie called a Tory? What did this term mean? Were there many Tories living in the colonies at this time? Have the students share their findings with the class.

5 When the story ends, Katie has not told her family what happened while she was inside the house. Her father, mother, brother, and sister do not know that John Warren saved her life by leading away the rebels. Have two groups of students role-play a scene in which Katie reveals to her family what happened. How will Katie tell her story? How will the various family members react?

6 Katie hid her sister's doll beneath the sofa. Colonial toys were different from today's toys. Invite two interested students, with help from an adult volunteer, to locate pictures of colonial toys, including dolls, and share them with the class.

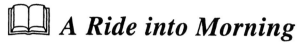 # *A Ride into Morning*

FICTION

by Ann Rinaldi

San Diego, CA: Harcourt Brace Jovanovich, 1991. 289p.

This book will appeal to fifth-grade readers. It is not illustrated. The story is told in the first person from the point of view of 14-year-old Mary Cooper.

Mary is outspoken about the cause of the Revolution. She has been sent away from her Tory family to live with her aunt and cousin, the Wicks, on their farm in Morristown. General Wayne and his troops winter on the Wicks' land.

Mary has made friends in camp with two young men, Jeremiah and David. From these boys, Mary learns that her cousin, Tempe, is seeing Billy Bowzar when she goes riding, and that General Wayne is afraid Bowzar may lead a mutiny because the men have not been paid or supplied with food.

Mary also learns that Tempe's brother, Henry, may not be insane, as everyone thinks.

Tempe cares for her mother and the farm, avoiding the politics of war. Each day, she rides her beautiful white horse, Colonel. The horse becomes a symbol for freedom. Bowzar tries to entice Tempe into loaning him Colonel, so that he may ride in style in the presence of General Wayne.

Tempe's sympathies drift away from the Revolution. Mary continues to be an ardent admirer of General Wayne and wants no part in compromise. When the troops mutiny, Tempe is forced to choose sides. She enacts a plan, conceived by her "lunatic" brother, to save Colonel, saving her integrity as well.

Discussion Starters and Multidisciplinary Activities

1 Tempe, throughout most of the story, believes in compromise. Have students discuss compromise. Are there times when people should compromise? Are there times when they shouldn't?

2 People go to doctors to be cured, yet Dr. Leddell states that "when a patient decides to help himself, he's three-quarters of the way to the cure." Have students discuss this statement.

3 At one point, Mary makes a statement about Colonel being a symbol for freedom. Have students discuss this statement. What role does the horse play in this story?

4 Have students who love horses and drawing make an illustration for the book that includes Colonel, identifying the page where the illustration should be placed. Display the drawings on a classroom bulletin board.

5 Invite a small group of students to role-play a scene from the book for the class. The scene selected should have interesting dialogue, but the students need not confine themselves to lines of dialogue as written; they may add dialogue for clarification and entertainment. The group might use costumes and simple props to enhance the presentation.

6 The dog in this story is named Oliver Cromwell. Have a pair of students research this man. Who was he? For what is he famous? Is it befitting that the dog in this story has this name? Have the students share their findings with the class.

Samuel's Choice

 FICTION

by Richard Berleth
illustrated by James Watling
Niles, IL: Albert Whitman, 1990. 40p.

This picture book with full-color illustrations will appeal to second- and third-grade readers. When the story begins, the main character, Samuel, is 14 years old.

Samuel, a black slave owned by Master Isaac van Ditmas, a rich farmer, works in his master's flour mill in Brooklyn, New York. Samuel learns to row a boat and dreams how it would feel to be free as the gulls.

When the Sons of Liberty approach the van Ditmas's property, van Ditmas locks his slaves in the house. Sana, a slave who can read and write, tells the others about the Declaration of Independence. When General Washington arrives in New York, van Ditmas directs Samuel to take his wife and their daughters to Staten Island, to safety.

When the Patriots retreat past the farm one day, many of the slaves leave with the soldiers. Samuel decides to help the Americans by rowing them across a creek under enemy fire. Major Gist boards the boat and directs them to Washington's camp. When they land, Samuel becomes Gist's orderly.

Under cover of fog and rain, Samuel helps Washington's army retreat from Brooklyn to Manhattan. He takes the end of a long rope and rows his boat to the Manhattan shore. Using the rope as a guide, other boats follow.

Isaac van Ditmas is arrested for helping the British and forced to surrender all his property to the army of the Continental Congress. All his slaves are freed.

Discussion Starters and Multidisciplinary Activities

1 After the Sons of Liberty came, waving their flags, several slaves talked in the kitchen. They said, "Liberty ain't for Africans. . . . And it got nothin' to do with us." Have students discuss this statement. Why did some slaves have this opinion? Why did others think they could be free if they took a risk?

2 Sana, Toby, and Nathaniel went up the road past the farm and into the line of American soldiers. They did not ask Samuel to come with them. Have students discuss why the other slaves said that it was Samuel's choice whether to seek freedom.

3 Have students discuss why Sana, unable to swim, went with Samuel to take the rope across the river in the storm.

4 Samuel and the other slaves dreamed of freedom. Invite interested students to write a poem about freedom and what it might have meant to one of Isaac van Ditmas's slaves.

5 Have a small group of students research the Sons of Liberty. Who were they? Who were their leaders? When was the group formed? Did the group's existence continue throughout the Revolution, or were they absorbed into another group? Have the students share their findings with the class.

6 Have a small group of students use the information presented in the book to make a map showing Long Island and Manhattan Island. Gowanus Creek, Gowanus Bay, and the East River should be included, and students should mark Samuel's various boat trips on the map. Post the map on a classroom bulletin board.

📖 *A Spy in the King's Colony*

FICTION

by Lisa Banim
illustrated by Tatyana Yuditskaya
New York: Silver Moon Press, 1994. 76p.

This book is appropriate for readers in grades three through five. Full-page black-and-white illustrations complement the text.

The setting is Boston, Massachusetts, in 1775 during British occupation. The central character is 11-year-old Emily Parker, who is from a Patriot family. Her father, a doctor, often holds political meetings in their house at night.

As the story begins, Emily is going with her friend Maggie to deliver Johnnycakes to Maggie's relatives at the pier. It gets late, so Emily buys the cod she was sent for and starts home. Maggie runs ahead, but Emily is stopped and questioned by a British soldier. Emily's neighbor, Robert Babcock, comes to the rescue and walks Emily home.

Robert stays for supper. When Emily sees someone with a scar looking in the window of their house, she begins to wonder if Robert is a spy.

The man who looked in the window comes the next day to ask Emily's father to pull a tooth, and he asks questions. Emily sees Robert meeting the man in a local tavern. During her father's secret meeting of Patriots, Emily listens and learns that an important message must go to General Washington. Emily also discovers a spy hiding in their house, listening.

A Patriot warns them that the British are coming, and the Patriots scatter. Emily entrusts the message for Washington to Robert and learns to her relief that he is spying for the Patriots, not the British.

Discussion Starters and Multidisciplinary Activities

1 Because Emily often embellishes the truth when she tells a story, her relatives and friends are inclined to say that she has a vivid imagination and do not put much stock in her tales. Ask students if Emily was wrong in suspecting Robert to be a spy.

2 The members of Robert's family are Tories, but he is a Patriot. Have students discuss why members of the same family might have opposite opinions about political matters.

3 At first, Emily leaves to carry the note to General Washington herself, but she decides instead to entrust the note to Robert. Ask students to discuss why she decided to trust him.

4 The reader learns that help is coming to General Washington by way of a special mission to Fort Ticonderoga. Have a small group of students research how cannons were brought from Fort Ticonderoga to Washington. Have the students share their research with the class.

5 Emily was working on a sampler. Invite someone who has a sampler to visit the class and share it with students. After the visit, have students send a thank you letter to the guest.

6 Emily's father mentions to one of his patients that he could have stopped at the forge to have the blacksmith pull his tooth. Invite a group of students to research medicine in the early colonies. What sort of training did the doctors and dentists have? Have the students share their research with the class.

From *Exploring Our Country's History.* © 1998 Phyllis J. Perry. Teacher Ideas Press. (800) 237-6124.

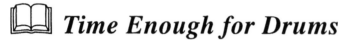 # *Time Enough for Drums*

FICTION

by Ann Rinaldi
New York: Holiday House, 1986. 249p.

This book will appeal to fourth- and fifth-grade readers. Other than the cover design, it has no illustrations. The story is told in the first person from the viewpoint of 15-year-old Jemima Emerson.

The Emerson family lives in a comfortable house in Trenton, New Jersey, where Mr. Emerson manages a store. Trenton is a divided community, with the Tories being loyal to the king, and the Patriots wanting a free and independent country. The Emersons support the Patriots.

Jemima, or Jem, is tutored by John Reid. She dislikes her tutor and proves to be a difficult pupil. Her mother is secretly writing articles for the newspaper in support of the Patriots. Her father will not sell taxed tea in his store. Her two brothers join the Patriot army, as does her good friend Raymond Moore, a Quaker.

Jem's brother Dan is a brave officer, and her brother David fights and is killed in a Patriot battle. Raymond Moore also dies. Jem is astonished to learn that John Reid is not a Tory after all, but a spy for General Washington. Eventually, he joins the army as well.

Jem must cope with having her town and home occupied by the British and Hessians, with her Tory sister, with her father's death, with the depression and illness of her mother, with managing the store, and with the battle of Trenton. She survives and eventually marries her tutor.

Discussion Starters and Multidisciplinary Activities

1   At what point in the story did students suspect that John Reid was not a Tory? What clues suggested that he supported the Patriots?

2   At what point in the story did students suspect that David Emerson would be killed in battle? What clues suggested that anger would lead him recklessly into battle?

3   Canoe is an interesting character. Encourage students to discuss the role that he plays in the story.

4   In the author's notes, John Fitch, a Trenton Patriot, is credited as being an inventor of the steamboat. Have a small group of interested students research this topic and the early history of steamboats. Have the students share their research with the class.

5   Canoe gave Jem some pemmican. Have a small group of students research pemmican. What is it made of? What makes it last? What people in the United States used pemmican?

6   General Washington led a surprise attack by crossing the ice-clogged Delaware River. Have students conduct an experiment to determine whether soil or water heats faster: Fill a jar half-full with soil; fill another jar half-full with water. Insert a thermometer into each substance (just below the surface) and tape it in place. Compare the temperatures after a few minutes. If the water is cooler or warmer than the soil, add warm or cool water until the temperatures are the same. Place a heat lamp over each jar (each jar should receive the same amount of light and heat). Record the temperatures every two minutes. Which substance heats faster?

◆ *Bridges and Poetry* ◆

 *Doodle Dandy!
The Complete Book
of Independence
Day Words*

 *The Winter of
Red Snow*

📖 *Year-Round
Programs for
Young Players*

BRIDGES
AND POETRY

📖 *Doodle Dandy!*
The Complete Book of
Independence Day Words

by Lynda Graham Barber
illustrated by Betsy Lewin
New York: Bradbury Press, 1992. 122p.

This book with humorous black-and-white line drawings will appeal to students in grades three through five.

Doodle Dandy! is filled with interesting bits of information that in some way relate to Independence Day. In a succinct format, it answers many questions that students may have: Who was the original "Uncle Sam"? How did the United States of America get its name? Who was the model for the Statue of Liberty? Why did Yankee Doodle call the feather in his cap "macaroni"?

This book also provides information about such historical events as the writing of our national anthem, the choice of the bald eagle as our national symbol, the design of the Great Seal of the United States, and the writing of the inscription on the Liberty Bell, and briefly describes some of the major battles of the American War of Independence. Eighteenth-century revolutions that took place around the world are briefly discussed. Information about how we celebrate the Fourth of July, including various types of fireworks and the history of barbecues and picnics, is provided.

Many words important to understanding the American Revolution are defined, such as *boycott, colony, representation, alarm, Patriots, Redcoats, mercenaries, revolutionary, Founding Fathers, pledge, liberty,* and *declaration.* Parts of patriotic poems are included, as well as the full text of the Declaration of Independence.

Possible Topics for Further Investigation

1 Flag Day is celebrated on June 14. Invite a small committee of students to research the changes in our country's flag. They should locate accurate pictures and dates of the changes throughout history. Each committee member should choose an historical flag and depict it in color, using any medium. Each depiction should be dated with the year the design was introduced. Display the complete set of flags on a classroom bulletin board.

2 One of the most famous poems by Walt Whitman is "Paul Revere's Ride." Have a small group of students obtain a copy of the poem and divide it into sections to study. Students may need to look up particular words to fully understand the poem. They should practice reading it aloud, with each student reading one section. Together, the group should select patriotic background music. When the group is ready, have the students record the poem and background music on audiocassette. Have the group play their recording for the class.

3 Some of the symbols for the United States, such as the bald eagle, are mentioned in the book. Your state probably has a number of symbols, such as a state bird, animal, flower, or tree. Invite two students to investigate the symbols of your state and the bordering states. Why was each symbol selected? Have the students share their findings with the class.

The Winter of Red Snow

by Kristiana Gregory
New York: Scholastic, 1996. 173p.

This book is part of the Dear America series, which presents events in American history in the form of fictional diaries. The book takes the form of a Revolutionary War diary of 13-year-old Abigail Jane Stewart, written at Valley Forge, Pennsylvania, in 1777. It will appeal to readers in grades three through five.

The first diary entry discloses that Abigail's mother is giving birth to a son. Mrs. Stewart has three healthy daughters but has lost six sons, all of whom died before reaching one year of age. The family is concerned about the new baby boy named John Edward.

In the entries that follow, the reader learns that General Washington is housed nearby. Mrs. Stewart does his washing, and Abigail and her older sister, Elizabeth, carry the laundry back and forth. They meet Mrs. Washington when she comes to stay with the General for four months. In her company, they visit soldiers who are sick and dying. They also see many important men who come to see the General.

The troops are camped at Valley Forge in tents and huts. They are poorly clothed and hungry. The girls sew a shirt and coat to give the soldiers. It is a constant problem for the residents that the soldiers steal food and other needed items. Through the diary entries, the reader learns that the troops are finally clothed, trained, and ready the following spring to march, looking like an army instead of scarecrows.

Possible Topics for Further Investigation

1. The small sketches on page 160 of the book depict the typical attire of people who lived in the 1700s. Invite interested students working with the media specialist or an adult volunteer to research the attire of men and women during this period, locating color illustrations if possible. The students should prepare a bibliography of all the resources used and should make sketches or (with permission) photocopy some of the pictures. Have the students share their findings with the class.

2. Many of the soldiers who wintered at Valley Forge died of smallpox. Have a group of students research smallpox vaccine. Who developed the vaccine? When? Is the vaccine still used? When and where were there epidemics of smallpox throughout the world? Ask these students to prepare a written report with bibliography sharing what they learn.

3. The noise from the fifes and drums wakes the baby, but Abigail likes the music better than the sounds of guns and cannons. Have a music specialist locate audiocassettes, records, or CDs that have military music from this period. Ask the specialist to share selected music with the class and to lead a discussion on the topic of military music.

 *Year-Round Programs for Young Players*

BRIDGES AND POETRY

by Aileen Fisher
Boston: Plays, 1985. 334p.

This book is suitable for use in grades three through five. It contains 100 plays, skits, poems, choral readings, recitations, and pantomimes for celebrating holidays and special occasions throughout the year. The book is divided into 12 sections, one for each month of the year. Production notes include suggestions for staging the plays simply, as well as suggestions for settings, costumes, and properties that students themselves can make.

In conjunction with a study of the 1700s in American history, the following will be of particular interest: "Benjamin Franklin's Birthday," "A Dish of Green Peas," "George Washington," "Washington Marches On," "How to Spell a Patriot," "Washington at Valley Forge," "The Many Rides of Paul Revere," "Long May It Wave," "A Star for Old Glory," "The Red, White, and Blue," "Old Glory," "Our Great Declaration," "Ask Mr. Jefferson," "My Bet on the Declaration," and "Thank You, America."

Also included are many spirited ideas for planning special classroom activities throughout the year, for Back to School Night, Halloween, Thanksgiving, Christmas, New Year's Day, Valentine's Day, Groundhog Day, Lincoln's Birthday, Washington's Birthday, St. Patrick's Day, Easter, Election Day, Martin Luther King Jr. Day, and Book Week.

Discussion Starters and Multidisciplinary Activities

1 Ask students to read and study four flag poems from the book and then discuss which is their favorite and why.

2 Thomas Jefferson was the major writer of the Declaration of Independence but is famous for other reasons, too. Ask a pair of students to research Jefferson and to make an oral report to the class on what they learn.

3 With a parent volunteer, arrange time for 14 students to rehearse and present the play "Our Great Declaration" for the remainder of the class. "Ask Mr. Jefferson" would involve another five students.

4 With additional volunteer help, have a group of students practice presenting "Thank You, America" as a choral reading. Arrange to share this with another class.

5 Encourage students to write original patriotic poems. Publish these in a class book using desktop publishing software. Students should include decorative patriotic symbols.

6 Have a group of older students write a play commemorating an American holiday or historical event. Students should select a holiday or event, outline the play, and determine the characters and their roles. The play should be drafted by one student, then edited as a group. Students should choose roles, make simple costumes and props, and present the play to an audience.

The 1700s

Nonfiction Connections

- *The American Revolution: How We Fought the War of Independence*
- *The Ben Franklin Book of Easy and Incredible Experiments*
- *Book of the New American Nation*
- *The Boston Tea Party*
- *The Fall of Quebec and the French and Indian War*
- *If You Were There in 1776*
- *A Multicultural Portrait of the American Revolution*
- *Paul Revere*
- *A Picture Book of George Washington*
- *The Revolutionary War: A Sourcebook on Colonial America*
- *A Young Patriot: The American Revolution As Experienced by One Boy*

The American Revolution: How We Fought the War of Independence

NONFICTION CONNECTIONS

by Edward F. Dolan
Brookfield, CT: Millbrook Press, 1995. 110p.

This large-format book with black-and-white illustrations is appropriate for third to fifth graders. It contains eight chapters, an index, and a bibliography.

Chapter 1 discusses April 19, 1775, when 70 men stood on the village green in Lexington, Massachusetts, waiting for British soldiers on their way to Concord. When the first shot rang out, the Revolutionary War began. The British marched on to Concord, and more shots were fired.

Chapter 2 describes the Navigation Acts, the Stamp Act, the Quartering Act, and the tea tax. Chapter 3 discusses the minutemen, who hid along the roads of Concord, following and firing upon the British troops as they left the city; the establishment of a Continental Congress; and the Battle of Bunker Hill.

Chapter 4 describes how Washington began to shape his men into an army while waiting for cannons from Fort Ticonderoga. When the cannons arrived, the British left Boston. Included is a description of the drafting of the Declaration of Independence.

Chapters 5 and 6 describe the war campaigns of the American Revolution from 1776 to 1778, including General Carleton on Lake Champlain, General Howe at New York, Washington at Trenton, Burgoyne's Campaign, St. Leger's Campaign, and Howe's Philadelphia Campaign. Chapters 7 and 8 discuss Valley Forge; the first victories of the American navy; and the battle at Yorktown, when Cornwallis surrendered in October 1781, marking the last major battle of the Revolution.

Possible Topics for Further Investigation

1 Have a small group of interested students, working with an adult volunteer or a library media specialist, obtain a copy of *Common Sense*, written by Thomas Paine and printed in 1776. Have the students prepare a presentation to share with the class. They might want to read aloud parts of the document, or they might prefer to summarize its main points. The students should share some information about Thomas Paine. Who was he? Where did he live? Why did he write this pamphlet?

2 The book describes many women who played a colorful part in our country's history. Invite a group of students to work in pairs to make a class book titled "Women Who Contributed During the Revolutionary War." Students should consult at least one source in addition to *The American Revolution*. The students should obtain pictures, drawings, or photocopies (if copyright allows) and document the special contributions of these women. The women discussed might included Abigail Adams, Sybil Ludington, Betsy Ross, and Molly Pitcher.

3 John Jay was one of the three participants from the United States who negotiated the Treaty of Paris, officially ending the Revolutionary War. Jay was also appointed the first chief justice of the United States Supreme Court. Have a group of students research the Supreme Court and share their findings with the class. What is the main function of the court? How many justices are there at present? What are the names of the people who currently serve on the court? How long do they serve? What is the process for appointing the justices?

The Ben Franklin Book of Easy and Incredible Experiments

Lisa Jo Rudy, Ed.
New York: John Wiley, 1995. 133p.

This Franklin Institute Science Museum Book contains material provided by the Institute staff and will appeal to students in grades three through five. Black-and-white drawings complement the text.

The experiments and activities in this book are divided into six topics: "Using Your Head" (observation), "Exploring the Weather," "Exciting Electricity," "Making Music," "Paper and Printing," and "Exploring Light and Sight." Additional information about Benjamin Franklin, and information about the Franklin Institute Science Museum, is provided.

Each section contains detailed instructions about how to make scientific observations, how to make simple scientific instruments, and how to conduct scientific investigations. Lists of materials and step-by-step procedures are included. In "Exploring the Weather," for example, students learn how to make an anemometer to measure the wind and a hygrometer to measure the water in the air. "Exciting Electricity" explains how to make an electroscope and how to experiment with static electricity. "Making Music" explains how to make bottle pipes and panpipes, a kazoo, and simple string instruments. In "Paper and Printing," students learn how to make letterpress stamps and a letterpress. In "Exploring Light and Sight," students learn how to make a prism, a kaleidoscope, and a periscope, and discover how light travels. Each section ends with a "What Next?" segment, which contains lists of additional books to guide students in learning more about each topic.

Possible Topics for Further Investigation

1. Have a pair of students write to the Franklin Institute Science Museum (20th & The Parkway, Philadelphia, PA 19103-1194), requesting pamphlets and other available information about the founding and history of the museum. Students should proofread their letter before preparing a final copy, and should include a 9-by-12-inch envelope, with enough postage for 3 ounces, self-addressed to one of the students. Any materials received should be shared with the class.

2. Have students conduct the first experiment in the book, discussed on pages 8 and 9, and compare their results with those of Franklin. Needed are several small squares of cloth, of the same fabric, in a range of solid colors from black to white. Place the squares flat on shaved ice in a baking pan. Set the pan in direct sunlight, or under a heat lamp. What happens to the ice beneath each color of cloth? Franklin found that the ice beneath the black and the dark-blue cloth melted faster than the ice beneath the white cloth.

3. Divide the class into teams to conduct a unit about exploring the weather. Have the teams make a complete weather station. Each group should be assigned to research and make one of the following instruments: a wind vane, an anemometer, a barometer, a hygrometer, a rain catcher, and a thermometer. Directions for making the instruments are included in *The Ben Franklin Book of Easy and Incredible Experiments*.

 *Book of the New American Nation*

by Marlene Smith-Baranzini and Howard Egger-Bovet
Boston: Little, Brown, 1995. 94p.

This large-format book with black-and-white illustrations will appeal to readers in grades three through five. It is part of the Brown Paper School USKids History series. Many of the events described take place in the late 1700s, although some take place in the 1800s.

The book is divided into a number of sections, with several stories, articles, games, and projects in each section: "The Plowboy and His Book: A Wild Mississippi Scheme"; "Living on Someone Else's Land"; "Jason's Secret"; "The First Inauguration"; "America's 'First Granddaughter'"; "Benjamin Banneker Surveys the Capital"; "A Trip with Father"; "One Step from Death"; "The Capitol Is Burning"; "The Longest Ditch in the World"; "Stolen Freedom on the Prairie"; "How a Long House Was Built"; "A Frontier Town"; "Little School on the Prairie"; "A Game: Do You Trust Me?"; "A Wedding at Bonneau's Plantation"; "The People's Choice"; "The Trail Where They Wept"; "The Land of White Gold"; "Hannie's First Week"; "Jason and the Mustangs"; and "Audubon's Assistant."

This book captures the excitement in our country that occurred after the colonists won their war for independence. There were flatboats traveling on the Ohio and Mississippi Rivers, settlers plowing land in the Ohio Territory, and people gathering in Philadelphia to form a new government. Land was surveyed for the nation's new capital. The Erie Canal was built. Our third president made the Louisiana Purchase and sent out explorers.

Possible Topics for Further Investigation

1. Several projects are explained in detail in *Book of the New American Nation*. Divide the class into seven groups and assign each a project. Suggested projects: Build a model flatboat; make a board game; play "The Cabinet Game," "Shuffling the Brogue," or "Do You Trust Me?"; make a mill doll; learn to spin a rope. Groups who make board games or learn to play games should teach them to the class. Other groups should demonstrate their skills (e.g., spinning a rope) or display their projects (e.g., model flatboat, mill doll).

2. Have an art educator from your school plan a lesson for students based on the material presented on page 85 of the book, under "Audubon's Assistant." Students should make clear acetate grids, place a grid in front of a flower specimen that is pinned inside the cover of a shoebox, and try to accurately draw the flower on an identical grid on a sheet of white drawing paper. Colored pencils or paints might be used to complete the picture.

3. The 363-mile Erie Canal opened in 1825, from Albany through Syracuse to Buffalo. A total of 83 locks were used to guide boats through the drop in elevation from Lake Erie to the Hudson River. Have a small group of students research the Erie Canal and share their findings with the class. They should use a map to trace its route and build a model to demonstrate how a lock operates. The students should also research how the Erie Canal, which became a part of the State Barge Canal System in 1918, is still used for recreational purposes today.

📖 *The Boston Tea Party*

by R. Conrad Stein
Danbury, CT: Childrens Press, 1996. 32p.

This book, part of the Cornerstones of Freedom series, will appeal to readers in grades two through four. Sketches and photographs complement the text.

The book begins with a discussion of the French and Indian War of 1763. After the war, England claims ownership of Canada and the region to the west of the 13 colonies. Because the war was costly, Britain is in debt. To rebuild its treasury, the British Parliament decides to tax the American colonies.

The Stamp Act is passed in 1765. This stirs anti-British feelings in the colonies. The British government stations two regiments of soldiers in Boston in 1768. In March 1770, citizens taunt a British soldier, who calls for help. Other soldiers come and shots are fired. Five Bostonians are killed.

News of the event, called the Boston Massacre, spreads throughout the colonies. Boston leads the protest against the tea tax. Britain gives the British East India Company a monopoly on selling tea in America. When three ships sail into Boston Harbor, the colonists refuse to unload their ships.

The governor sets a date by which taxes must be paid. A crowd meets, and 50 men disguised as Mohawks go aboard the ships and dump the tea. As a result, King George places Massachusetts under military control. Delegates from the other colonies form the first Continental Congress. The Boston Tea Party sets into motion a chain of events that results in America's independence.

Possible Topics for Further Investigation

1. The Adams family name is mentioned often throughout the book. Samuel Adams was born in Boston in 1722 and was an enthusiastic anti-British spokesperson. In Massachusetts, he helped organize the Committees of Correspondence and the Sons of Liberty. His cousin, John Adams, also became a convert to the cause of independence and became the second president of the United States. The writings of Abigail Adams, wife to John Adams, provide interesting viewpoints. The son of John and Abigail, John Quincy Adams, became our sixth president. Invite a group of students to research the Adams family, write a report (citing sources of information), and post the report in the classroom.

2. The report of the Boston Tea Party is presented vividly in the book. Have interested students role-play what happened. One or two students should describe what happened that night in Boston Harbor to two interested people who watched the action from the docks. The observers should ask questions. Have the students include a description of what happened to John Crane. Have students practice the dialogue and then share the presentation with the class.

3. The tea tax was particularly upsetting to the colonists, but it was only one of many taxes and acts levied upon the colonists by the British Parliament. Invite a small group of interested students to research these taxes and acts. They should make a large chart that indicates the names of the taxes and acts, the dates on which they were enacted, and a brief description of how each tax or act affected the colonists. Post the chart on a classroom bulletin board.

From *Exploring Our Country's History.* © 1998 Phyllis J. Perry. Teacher Ideas Press. (800) 237-6124.

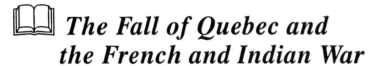

The Fall of Quebec and the French and Indian War

NONFICTION CONNECTIONS

by George Ochoa
Englewood Cliffs, NJ: Silver Burdett, 1990. 64p.

This book, divided into four chapters, is appropriate for fourth- and fifth-grade readers. A few maps and pictures supplement the text.

Chapter 1, "The Rivals in the New World," discusses rivalries in early America. In 1534, Jacques Cartier explored the Gulf of the St. Lawrence for France. Spain was making settlements in New Mexico and Florida. At about the same time, the Dutch settled in New York, and the English settled in New England.

Chapter 2, "The Endless War," begins with a discussion of the Schenectady Massacre. Four wars were fought between 1689 and 1697, with brief periods of peace between them. As a group, these are called the French and Indian Wars. The French built a line of forts between Lake Erie and the Ohio River and refused to leave. When George Washington and his men reached the Ohio Valley, they were defeated.

Chapter 3, "The Battle for Empire," describes the many actions taken to drive out the French when William Pitt came to power as the new British minister in 1757. He raised money and supplied the troops. Great Britain encroached upon Quebec.

Chapter 4, "The End of an Empire," describes the fall of Quebec. In September 1759, the British light infantry climbed the 175-foot-high protective cliffs and killed, captured, and chased away the sentries. General Wolfe then defeated the Marquis de Montcalm's army and, on September 18, 1759, Quebec surrendered.

Possible Topics for Further Investigation

1 The French and Indian Wars put Great Britain in possession of Canada and left a population of French-speaking Canadians who have struggled to keep their identity in a country where English is the predominant language. In the 1990s, an election was held in which French-speaking Canadians tried to obtain enough votes to secede from Canada and form a separate country. The vote failed, but the problem lingers. Have a group of students, working with a media specialist and using the *Readers' Guide to Periodical Literature*, read various magazine articles to investigate how French-speaking Canadians have dealt with this problem. Have students share their findings with the class.

2 The Treaty of Paris of 1783 officially ended the war between the United States and Great Britain and defined the border between the United States and Canada. Today, this boundary is the longest undefended border in the world. Have a group of students work with an adult volunteer to research the border. What is required for an American to cross the border into Canada on vacation? What questions will be asked of the tourist? How long may the tourist remain? Do the same regulations apply to Canadians who wish to visit the United States? Have students share what they learn with the class.

3 An American can briefly visit Canada by walking across the bridge at Niagara Falls. Have a group of students research this spot and obtain pictures of Niagara Falls and the bridge to share with the class.

📖 *If You Were There in 1776*

by Barbara Brenner
New York: Macmillan Books for Young Readers, 1994. 136p.

This book will appeal to students in grades three through five. It is divided into 17 chapters and contains black-and-white illustrations throughout.

This book begins by describing what it was like in the world of 1776: Napoleon is only 7, George III rules England, Gainsborough is painting portraits, and James Watt has invented the steam engine. Exciting things are happening.

Three million people are living in North America; of these, 2 million live in the 13 British colonies. Although there are many differences among the colonies, all have a common background, similar governments, and resent royal governors and taxes. Colonists hold grievance meetings and protests. In 1775, Washington assumed a position as general of the Continental army. Battles at Lexington and Concord have already been fought.

Later chapters discuss the clothing that people wore in 1776, as well as common foods and beverages. Chapters are devoted to farmers, planters, cities, playtime, religion, arts and crafts, and Native Americans. A chapter about the frontier in America describes settlers heading north into Maine and west to Kentucky. A chapter about the enslaved explains what life was like for the black population.

Of particular interest is a chapter devoted to a discussion of the writing of the Declaration of Independence, highlighting the arguments among the delegates and explaining that several delegates abstained from voting because they opposed the document.

Possible Topics for Further Investigation

1. Most students will be familiar with the names of Thomas Jefferson and George Washington and will know of their contributions to the struggle for independence. They will probably know considerably less about Arthur Middleton, Peyton Randolph, Richard Henry Lee, John Rutledge, and George Mason. Invite 10 students to work in pairs to research these five men. Each student pair should write a brief report about the person, including a bibliography listing at least two sources of information.

2. Although Jewish people settled in Newport, Rhode Island, long ago, they were not allowed to vote in 1776. Encourage interested students to write letters to the editor of a popular newspaper of the time, the *Newport Mercury*, urging a change in the law to give Jews voting rights. What arguments should be presented? Could the same arguments that were presented to secure freedoms from Great Britain be used to support pleas for the rights of Jewish people to vote? Post the letters on a classroom bulletin board.

3. Invite students to draw original pictures about life in 1776 to add to a classroom bulletin board. Pictures should be drawn on 18-by-24-inch posterboard, and each should have a brief caption. Scenes might depict the signing of the Declaration of Independence, children playing marbles, slaves picking cotton, a church service, General Washington on his horse, Molly Pitcher at her cannon, and so on.

From *Exploring Our Country's History*. © 1998 Phyllis J. Perry. Teacher Ideas Press. (800) 237-6124.

📖 *A Multicultural Portrait of the American Revolution*

NONFICTION CONNECTIONS

by Fran Zell
New York: Benchmark Books, 1996. 80p.

This book is suitable for fourth- and fifth-grade readers. It contains black-and-white and color illustrations. Events and topics related to the American Revolution are discussed from not only the perspective of the white European Americans but also the perspective of ethnic minorities, such as African Americans, Asian Americans, Hispanic Americans, and Native Americans.

Chapter 1, "Trouble Brews: Strained Relations with England," discusses the various taxes on the colonies, the Boston Massacre, the Boston Tea Party, colonial women who helped the cause, the antislavery sentiment, and violence on the frontier.

Chapter 2, "On the Eve of Revolution: A Changing People," examines the rich and poor among the colonists, the rural and city life of the colonies, indentured servants, limits on women's rights, the push westward, the varied cultures of the American Indians, and Africans suffering under slavery.

Chapter 3, "Unleashing Freedom's Cry," describes the roles of blacks at Lexington and Concord, at Bunker Hill, and in the Continental army in 1777. Also discussed is the role of Native Americans in the struggle between the British and the Americans.

Chapter 4, "The War Drags On (1776 to 1780)," explains how foreign forces helped the Americans.

Chapter 5, "Freedom Rings, but Not for All," explains that even after independence, America contained many people who did not have equal rights and freedoms.

Possible Topics for Further Investigation

1 Phillis Wheatley was an African slave who became world famous as a poet about 1770. Her Boston owners bought her from a slave ship in 1761, schooled her, recognized her talents, and helped her through the publishing process. Several biographies and collections of her poetry are available. Have a few students research Phillis Wheatley. They should read some of her poetry, choose a few selections that they particularly admire, and read these selections to the class.

2 Have a group of students make a game, "Revolutionary War Personalities," for the class to play: Students should use 3-by-5-inch index cards or colored file cards, writing the names of famous figures (e.g., Crispus Attucks) on the fronts and the events for which the figures are remembered on the back ("Killed in the Boston Massacre, March 5, 1770—first confrontation between colonists and British resulting in death"). Divide the deck of cards into six stacks, with the names of figures face-up. Players take turns, rolling a die. If a *3* is rolled, for example, the player must name the event for which the personality from the top card of stack three is remembered. A player who answers correctly keeps the card. A player who answers incorrectly must place the card at the bottom of the stack. The player with the most cards at end of the playing period wins.

3 Chapter 3 discusses how Native Americans were persuaded to help the British or the colonists. Invite a group of students to make two charts, one listing the tribes or nations that supported the British, the other listing the tribes or nations that supported the colonists. Post the charts on a classroom bulletin board.

 *Paul Revere*

by Martin Lee
New York: Franklin Watts, 1987, 96p.

This book, part of the First Book Biographies series, is appropriate for readers in grades four and five. It is divided into 12 chapters.

Chapter 1 discusses the life of Apollos Rivorie, who at 13 comes to America as an apprentice to a silversmith in Boston. Apollos grows up, marries, and has a son named Paul Revere.

Chapters 2, 3, and 4 document the early years of Paul Revere growing up in a thriving port city, going to school, and learning to be a silversmith. When his father dies, Paul manages the business. In 1756, at age 21, Paul joins the army for one year to fight against the French and Indians.

Chapters 5, 6, and 7 discuss the unrest and rebellion in Boston against British taxation. Revere becomes a member of the Sons of Liberty. When several shiploads of tea arrive in Boston harbor, Revere rides to port towns to give warning. After the famous Boston Tea Party, he rides to New York and Philadelphia to tell the news.

Chapters 8, 9, and 10 discuss the British blockade of Boston and the military presence. As the British plan to take supplies from Concord, the colonists establish a signal system of lanterns to be placed in North Church. Revere spreads the alarm by riding to Lexington. Halfway to Concord, he is captured, but then later released. Revere continues to help the cause by making cannons, gunpowder, and copper sheeting for ships.

Possible Topics for Further Investigation

1   As a boy, Paul Revere organized a group of bell-ringers. They formed a society and rang the bells at Christ Church. As a man, he made more than 400 bells, including one which still hangs in King's Chapel in Boston. Invite a small group of students to determine if any of the churches or other buildings in your town or city have bells. If so, the students should arrange a visit at a time when they can see the bells and ask questions about them. Where and when were the bells manufactured? How big are they? Have students share their findings with the class.

2   Although he was originally a silversmith, Paul Revere is well known for his work with copper. Revere made the copper sheathing for the famous American warship the *Constitution*. Have a small group of students research this warship and share their findings with the class. When and where was the *Constitution* active in battle? Where is the warship kept now? Are pamphlets available describing the size of the ship?

3   Another project in which Paul Revere was involved was Robert Fulton's steamship. Have a group of interested students research this topic. Who was Robert Fulton? When and where did he live? What was the importance of the steamship he built? When was the Fulton steamship built and where was it used? Have the students prepare a written report, including a bibliography of sources consulted. Have the group present a brief oral report to the class.

From *Exploring Our Country's History.* © 1998 Phyllis J. Perry. Teacher Ideas Press. (800) 237-6124.

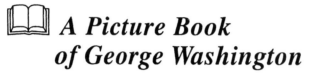

A Picture Book of George Washington

by David A. Adler
illustrated by John Wallner and Alexandra Wallner
New York: Holiday House, 1989. 32p. (unnumbered)

This book will appeal to students in kindergarten through third grade. It consists mostly of full-page color drawings, supplemented with minimal text.

The book begins with George Washington's birth on February 22, 1732, in the English colony of Virginia. He is pictured as a young man who enjoys fishing, boating, and horseback riding. In school, George's favorite subject was arithmetic.

George was only 11 when his father died. He helped his mother manage the farm and learned to use surveying tools that had belonged to his father. By the time he was 16, he had been given a job to survey land in the Virginia wilderness.

When he was 21, George joined the Virginia army. In 1754, George participated in the French and Indian War fighting on the side of England. He gained a reputation as a good leader.

He married Martha Custis when he was 26, and they lived in Mount Vernon, Virginia. In April 1775, fighting erupted when the American colonies refused to pay taxes to England. The leaders of the colonies met in Philadelphia and chose George to lead the Continental army in the Revolutionary War. The army was poor, lacking food, blankets, and guns.

Eight years later, when the war ended, George came home a hero and was elected the first president of the United States of America. He served two terms and then retired to Mount Vernon. George Washington died in 1799.

Possible Topics for Further Investigation

1   Have the class make a time line of Washington's life. Eight sets of important dates for the time line are included on the last page of the book. Have an adult volunteer obtain eight sheets of 36-inch-wide roller paper and help groups of students (approximately three students each) enter the dates and descriptions across the top of a sheet of paper. Have each group make a drawing beneath the description, showing George Washington in action at that stage of his life. Hang the eight sheets in chronological order across one wall of the classroom.

2   Washington's favorite subject in school was arithmetic. Invite a small group of students to conduct a survey to determine favorite school subjects. An adult volunteer might design and photocopy a small ballot that notes "Check your favorite subject:" and then lists a variety a subjects, including math, reading, science, and social studies. With permission from classroom teachers, have students distribute and collect ballots from all first-, second-, and third-grade classes. Have the students graph the results for each grade level.

3   Washington used to ride north of Mount Vernon to watch the building of Washington, the new capital of the United States. One of the men responsible for designing the city was Benjamin Banneker. Invite a small group of students, working with a media specialist or an adult volunteer, to research Benjamin Banneker. Have students share their findings with the class.

📖 The Revolutionary War: A Sourcebook on Colonial America

■
**NONFICTION
CONNECTIONS**

edited by Carter Smith
Brookfield, CT: Millbrook Press, 1991. 96p.

This book, part of the American Albums from the Collections of the Library of Congress, is divided into three parts. It is appropriate for students in grades four and five. Black-and-white photographs of documents from the Library of Congress complement the text.

Part 1 covers April 1775 to June 1776 and documents the fight for a new nation. When the war begins, many colonists do not want complete independence, but distrust of Parliament grows. In January 1776, Thomas Paine publishes a pamphlet, *Common Sense*, arguing for complete independence.

Part 2 covers July 1776 to February 1778. When the Declaration of Independence makes clear the motives for the war, battles begin in earnest. The colonists are at a disadvantage because the British have economic and military strength. The Continental army suffers defeats in the Battle of Long Island and in the capture of Fort Washington. The American victory at Saratoga is a major turning point in the Revolution. It prevents the British from isolating New England and encourages the French to join the Revolution.

Part 3 covers July 1778 to February 1783 and details the final battles of the Revolution and the diplomacy leading to the peace treaty. When the French ally themselves with the United States, they begin sending a supply of soldiers, ships, and money. When Cornwallis surrenders at Yorktown, it is clear that the British have been defeated. In September 1783, the Treaty of Paris is signed.

Possible Topics for Further Investigation

1. Involve the class in assembling a time line of the American Revolution. Helpful information can be found on pages 12–15, 40–43, and 64–67 of the book. Each student should choose one of the major events listed, then describe the event and its importance in American history on a 3-by-5-inch index card. Divide a sheet of roller paper into sections to show the time periods from April 1775 to February 1783, and hang the paper along a classroom wall. As students complete their cards, they should place them in the appropriate place along the time line.

2. During the American Revolution, some families found themselves divided over the issue of Independence. A wife might feel loyalty to the king while a husband wanted independence from Great Britain. One brother might be a Patriot and another a Tory. Have a group of students role-play a scene for the class in which a colonial family is gathered around the table arguing about the war for independence. Both viewpoints should be represented.

3. An old political cartoon appears on page 84 of the book. Political cartoons are still popular today. Have a group of interested students collect political cartoons from area newspapers for two weeks, posting them on a classroom bulletin board. Have the students each draw an original political cartoon about a current event or figure. Post the original cartoons on the bulletin board.

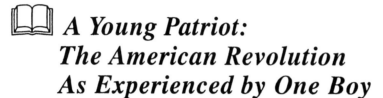

A Young Patriot: The American Revolution As Experienced by One Boy

by Jim Murphy
New York: Clarion Books, 1996. 101p.

This book, divided into eight chapters, is appropriate for third- through fifth-grade readers. The black-and-white illustrations were obtained from various historical archives. The book traces the history of Joseph Plumb Martin who was born in 1760 and raised by his grandparents in Connecticut.

Chapter 1, "The Smell of War," explains that even though Joseph is a child, he is aware of the actions of the Sons of Liberty. In Chapter 2, "Now I Was a Soldier," 14-year-old Joseph enlists as a soldier. In Chapter 3, "The Smell of Powder," he is outfitted for the army and goes to New York City for training. At Long Island, he gets his first taste of battle. Then he becomes ill and returns home.

Chapter 4, "Marching, Watching, Starving, and Freezing," describes the ordeals that the soldiers experience. In the spring of 1777, Joseph reenlists and is positioned at Peekskill. He fights at the Battle of Germantown and then goes to Fort Mifflin. After losing the fort, the men travel to Valley Forge.

Chapter 5, "Sending the Lobsterbacks Scurrying," describes the Battle of Monmouth. Chapter 6, "The War and Joseph Go South," describes the Battle of Yorktown. Chapter 7, "Parted Forever," reveals the beginning of the end of the war. A provisional peace treaty is signed on April 15, 1783. In Chapter 8, "A Cordial and Long Farewell," Joseph, now 22, is discharged and goes to Maine. At age 70, he publishes an account of his life as a soldier in the Revolution.

Possible Topics for Further Investigation

1 Have students study the pictures on pages 3 and 4 of the book. Although they depict the same event, they present the details in different ways, to arouse different sentiments in the viewer. Have a group of students look through several newspapers and clip out accounts and political cartoons depicting a current political event or figure. Have the students share these clippings and cartoons, explaining how they are exaggerated in specific ways to elicit a particular reaction.

2 Page 23 of the book shows a drawing of the world's first combat submarine, which became active in battle in 1776. Invite a group of interested students to research modern-day submarines. Who contributed to the design of the modern submarine? How big is a submarine? How many people can a submarine carry? When was a submarine last used in a war? Have students share their findings with the class.

3 Revolutionary soldiers were often without shoes, coats, and warm clothing. They suffered during the cold winters. As an activity related to temperature, have students make a thermometer: Fill one-eighth of a clear, narrow-neck plastic bottle (a volume of approximately 11 fluid ounces is recommended) with equal parts tap water and rubbing alcohol. Add a few drops of food coloring and stir. Put a clear plastic straw into the bottle, orienting the straw so that the end of the straw is submerged but not touching the bottom of the jar. With modeling clay, seal the neck of the jar, securing the straw in place. In a warm spot, the liquid will rise through the straw. In a cold spot, the liquid will drop.

Part III

THE 1800s

The 1800s

● FICTION ●

- 📖 *An American Army of Two*
- 📖 *The Blue and the Gray*
- 📖 *The Gentleman Outlaw and Me—Eli: A Story of the Old West*
- 📖 *If You Please, President Lincoln*
- 📖 *Mountain Valor*
- 📖 *Mr. Lincoln's Whiskers*

- 📖 *Pink and Say*
- 📖 *Reluctant Hero: A Snowy Road to Salem in 1802*
- 📖 *Wagons West!*
- 📖 *Washington City Is Burning*
- 📖 *Which Way Freedom?*

◆ BRIDGES AND POETRY ◆

- 📖 *Dear Levi: Letters from the Overland Trail*
- 📖 *For Home and Country: A Civil War Scrapbook*
- 📖 *Barbara Frietchie*

■ NONFICTION CONNECTIONS ■

- 📖 *Addy's Cook Book*
- 📖 *Children of the Westward Trail*
- 📖 *Civil War*
- 📖 *Explorers, Trappers, and Guides*
- 📖 *A House Divided: The Lives of Ulysses S. Grant and Robert E. Lee*
- 📖 *Jesse James*

- 📖 *John C. Fremont: Soldier and Pathfinder*
- 📖 *Lewis and Clark: Explorers of the American West*
- 📖 *Matthew Brady: His Life and Photographs*
- 📖 *The Mountain Men*
- 📖 *The Story of Clara Barton*

—OTHER TOPICS TO EXPLORE—

—Andrew Johnson	—Dred Scott	—Gold rush	—Stephen Austin
—Border states	—Factory system	—Railroads	—Telegraph
—Clipper ships	—Fourteenth Amendment	—Reconstruction	—Trent affair

From *Exploring Our Country's History*. © 1998 Phyllis J. Perry. Teacher Ideas Press. (800) 237-6124.

The 1800s

● *Fiction* ●

- 📖 *An American Army of Two*
- 📖 *The Blue and the Gray*
- 📖 *The Gentleman Outlaw and Me—Eli: A Story of the Old West*
- 📖 *If You Please, President Lincoln*
- 📖 *Mountain Valor*
- 📖 *Mr. Lincoln's Whiskers*
- 📖 *Pink and Say*
- 📖 *Reluctant Hero: A Snowy Road to Salem in 1802*
- 📖 *Wagons West!*
- 📖 *Washington City Is Burning*
- 📖 *Which Way Freedom?*

An American Army of Two

FICTION

by Janet Greeson
illustrated by Patricia Rose Mulvihill
Minneapolis, MN: Carolrhoda Books, 1992. 48p.

This book will appeal to readers in grades two and three. The book contains many full-color illustrations. The major characters are Rebecca and Abigail Bates.

The story begins in 1814. Congress declared war with England in 1812, so British sailors and American soldiers are enemies. Rebecca and Abigail help their father in a lighthouse. When two English ships sail into view headed for Cedar Point, the Bateses get into a small boat and row to shore in Scituate to alert the people. Most think they cannot fight because they are not soldiers. One of the townspeople rides in search of the Massachusetts Home Guard.

The British land in Scituate and demand meat, vegetables, and water. When the townspeople refuse to supply their enemies, the British burn some of their fishing boats and take others. Over the next few weeks, British land often and take food.

On one of their landings, the British hear the sounds of Yankee Doodle being played on fife and drum. Knowing that the Home Guard is approaching, the British sail away. One person is posted at the lighthouse to ride for help if the British return.

The member of the Home Guard teaches Rebecca and Abigail to play the fife and drum. When the British return weeks later and row toward shore, Abigail and Rebecca hide in the cedars and play the fife and drum. Thinking that soldiers are coming, the sailors turn their boats and leave, frightened away by an army of two.

Discussion Starters and Multidisciplinary Activities

1 When the Bates family warns the townspeople that the British are coming, one man rides in search of the Massachusetts Home Guard for protection. Have the students discuss whether the citizens could have done anything else. Why?

2 Have students discuss why they think Rebecca and Abigail learned to play the fife and drum. Did the girls learn to play just for fun or did they plan to use their musical skill in some way?

3 An author's note explains that fifers and drummers were important because, over the noise of battle, they passed on commands to march or charge or retreat. They were often young boys, and often a target for the enemy. Ask students if they would prefer to be a regular soldier in the army or a fifer or drummer. Why?

4 Enlist the aid of a music specialist to teach the students to sing "Yankee Doodle Dandy" and to learn to accompany the lyrics with sounds from simple musical instruments.

5 Most of America's early lighthouse keepers were men, but women, too, have held these positions. Invite a small group of students to research Abbie Burgess Grant, who is famous for her role in an 1856 storm that struck Matinicus Rock Lighthouse off the coast of Maine. Have students share their findings with the class.

6 Have a group of students, with help from a media specialist or an adult volunteer, make a map of the eastern coast of the United States. Students should mark the location of all existing lighthouses. Post the map in the classroom.

From *Exploring Our Country's History.* © 1998 Phyllis J. Perry. Teacher Ideas Press. (800) 237-6124.

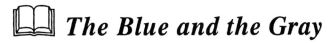 ## The Blue and the Gray

FICTION

by Eve Bunting
illustrated by Ned Bittinger
New York: Scholastic, 1996. 32p. (unnumbered)

This picture book is appropriate for students in kindergarten through third grade. Softly colored illustrations fill about three-fourths of each page. The narration is in the form of a long poem that makes use of end rhyme.

A young boy, his friend J. J. Huff, and the young boy's father share the excitement of watching the construction of their homes in a housing project. The homes are being built near grassy fields that were a Civil War battleground in 1862.

The young boy's father tells the two children about this war, in which the North fought against the South, the blue against the gray, white against white, and white against black. He points out a spot where the rebels and their horses hid. Their dog barks, and the sound is as sharp as the shots that were fired long ago.

The boys are surprised to learn that the general for the North and the captain for the South were once friends. The boys can't believe that friends and even brothers would ever fight against each other in a war.

J. J. remarks that it seems unfair that nothing has been placed in the field to mark the event and tell the story, but the boys and the father believe that perhaps their homes will be a monument of sorts. The boys promise to remember the story, even as they are sledding and playing ball where the men in blue and gray fought so long ago.

Discussion Starters and Multidisciplinary Activities

1. Ask students to point out the difference between this piece of land when it was a battleground and the present time when a new housing project is being built on the site.

2. The boy in this story and his friend J. J. say, "We'd never." Have students discuss this statement. What circumstances might cause two friends or two brothers to fight against each other?

3. Ask students if they think a housing subdivision is a worthy monument for a Civil War battleground. Should a traditional monument be installed in the area?

4. Ned Bittinger, the artist for the book, lives in Virginia at the foot of the Blue Ridge Mountains. Have a student locate these mountains on a map and point them out to classmates.

5. Have a small group of students study some of the flags that were flown over battlefields during the Civil War. Students should draw, label, and color these flags and display them in the classroom. The Union flag, the Confederate flag, and special flags of various divisions might be depicted.

6. The color blue is associated with the Union army. Have students conduct an experiment to learn about light and color: Set a large bowl of water by a window in direct sunlight. Submerge a small hand mirror in the water, tilting it toward the light. Position a sheet of white paper to catch the reflection from the mirror. A rainbow of colors will appear on the paper.

From *Exploring Our Country's History*. © 1998 Phyllis J. Perry. Teacher Ideas Press. (800) 237-6124.

FICTION

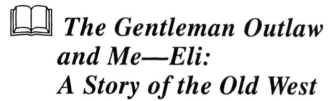

The Gentleman Outlaw and Me—Eli: A Story of the Old West

by Mary Downing Hahn
New York: Clarion Books, 1996. 212p.

This book will appeal to fourth- and fifth-grade readers. Except for the cover, it is without illustrations. The story is told in the first person from the point of view of a 12-year-old girl, Eliza (known as Eli), who is disguised as a boy during most of the story.

Eli's mother has died, and her father left some years ago to seek his fortune in Colorado. She decides to run away from abusive relatives to find her father. Eli dresses as a boy and takes with her a dog named Caesar.

They come upon a 17-year-old boy named Calvin Featherbone, who is on his way to Colorado to shoot the sheriff of Tinville, whom he blames for killing his father. The young man hopes to earn his way by cheating at cards; he says that he is known as the Gentleman Outlaw.

Calvin and Eli have a number of adventures. When luck is with them, they stay in fancy hotels and eat well. When Calvin cheats at cards and is discovered, they are run out of town with nothing. Constant enemies are Roscoe and Shovel Face.

On stolen horses, Calvin and Eli reach Tinville, where Calvin learns the truth about his father and Eli confesses that she's the daughter of Sheriff Yates. Eli helps her father identify Roscoe and picks Roscoe's pockets, giving money to Calvin, whom she releases from jail using stolen keys. Eli intends to remain in Tinville with her father and learn photography from Miss Jenny. Calvin goes to live with his grandfather and returns to school.

Discussion Starters and Multidisciplinary Activities

1   Eli's father had not abandoned her, as she had thought. He had faithfully sent letters and money to her, but her uncle kept this a secret. Ask students if they suspected this before it was revealed in the book. Why?

2   Eli knew that taking Caesar might cause problems. Actually, the dog proved helpful. Have students list what Caesar did that helped Eli on her journey.

3   Ask students whether they think Eli and Calvin will ever again meet. Why?

4   Have interested students trace Eli's journey on a map. Among the places mentioned are Clark Summit, Elms Bluff, and Dodge City (Kansas); and Pueblo, Denver, Alamosa, Durango, Silverton, Ouray, and Tinville (Colorado). Which of these towns and cities appear on the map? Have students share the route with the class.

5   One of the minor characters mentioned in the book is Doc Holliday. Have a small group of students research this colorful western figure and share their findings with the class. Where and when did Doc Holliday live? For what is he famous? How did he die?

6   The Durango & Silverton Narrow Gauge Railroad Company (with offices at 479 Main Ave., Durango, CO 81301) still carries tourists, providing a peek at early western life. Have a student write to the company for information. How long is the journey? How much does it cost? The student should include a self-addressed, stamped envelope with the letter of request and should share any information received with the class.

FICTION

If You Please,
President Lincoln

by Harriette Gillem Robinet

New York: Atheneum Books for Young Readers, 1995. 149p.

This book will appeal to fourth- and fifth-graders. Moses, the main character, is a 14-year-old slave. The book has no illustrations.

The story begins on Christmas Eve 1863. Aunt Rebekah is sick and old, but she prays that Moses will become free. Because Moses belongs to Father Fitzpatrick, who does not believe in freeing slaves, Moses is uncomfortable upon hearing his aunt's prayers. When Rebekah dies and Moses overhears Father Fitzpatrick planning to sell him for $800, Moses runs away.

He finds work and hides on Washington Wharf. When Father Fitzpatrick comes hunting him, Moses again runs. He is befriended by a blind black man named Goshen. In Annapolis, the two of them are welcomed aboard a Baltimore clipper. They find themselves part of a new plan for colonization. When they try to leave the ship, they are struck and kept aboard.

After a long journey, during which many of the slaves die, they reach Cow Island. Goshen, Moses, and the other passengers are left there, along with Governor Kock, who is responsible for the new colony. They are without water or food. They dig wells and try to survive by eating fish and whatever they can forage, but many die.

Moses travels about five miles across shark-invested waters in a barrel to reach Haiti and tell of their plight. He is thrown in jail, escapes, and returns to Cow Island. Eventually, a boat comes for them and takes the people to the United States. Moses and Goshen settle in the District of Columbia.

Discussion Starters and Multidisciplinary Activities

1   Although several hundred people made the trip to Cow Island, Moses was recognized as their leader, even though he was only a boy. Have students discuss this. What traits made Moses a natural leader?

2   Throughout the book, Moses resents the nickname Moz used by his friend Goshen. Have students discuss why Moses is so sensitive about his name and why he waits so long to complain to Goshen.

3   The crew of the ship that brings Moses and the others from Cow Island to the United States says awful things about them. Have students discuss why the crew spoke as they did.

4   People on Cow Island collected fresh rainwater in a barrel. Have students predict how many inches of rain fall during a typical rainstorm in your area, and then conduct an experiment to test the prediction: Place a large, clean coffee can on a flat, unprotected area outdoors. After a rainstorm, have students use a ruler to measure the depth of the water collected. Was the prediction accurate?

5   Moses said to his students, "Be prepared to fulfill our dreams." Have students make posters, based on this statement as a theme, in which they picture themselves as adult homemakers or professionals. Display the posters on a classroom bulletin board.

6   Moses had a button collection. If someone in your town has a button collection, invite the collector to visit the class and share the collection. Students should prepare appropriate questions before the visit. After the visit, have students send a thank you letter to the guest.

 *Mountain Valor*

by Gloria Houston
New York: Philomel, 1994. 239p.

This book will appeal to mature fifth-grade readers. It is told from the viewpoint of a 12-year-old girl, Valor, and is based on the true story of Matilda Houston. The book contains a few black-and-white sketches.

When the Civil War breaks out, Valor stays at home on the farm in North Carolina with her mother, Sarah, and her cousin, Jed. Helping to care for them are Savannah, a free black woman, and Ben, her husband. Valor's father and one brother join the Confederates. Another brother and her uncle are Union soldiers. Marauders from both armies come by the farm. One, a Union soldier with a red beard, causes Valor's pregnant mother to fall down the stairs and miscarry.

Valor raises a horse named Sam. As the years pass, she wants to be respected like a man. When the red-bearded man returns, killing Ben, wounding Jed, and taking Valor's horse and all the livestock, Valor pursues him disguised as a boy. She stops at the home of an old herbalist to get herbs that will render the soldiers unconscious if served in tea. Valor meets Randall, a cook for the soldiers, and goes with him to the Union camp. She drugs the soldiers and returns home with the livestock, disregarding a chance to kill the red-bearded man.

Valor is ill for weeks. Her father returns and is proud of his courageous daughter. Her relatives come home safely from the war and bring a message that Randall will soon visit.

Discussion Starters and Multidisciplinary Activities

1   Although Jed and Valor were competitive, they cared very much about each other. Have students point out and discuss examples from the book that show the competitiveness and love between Jed and Valor.

2   After Sarah miscarries, she is ill and does not come downstairs for years. Then she changes, almost overnight, becoming a strong and active woman again. Have students discuss this transformation. Was it believable?

3   When Valor had the opportunity to kill the red-bearded man, she chose not to do so. Have students discuss her decision.

4   Randall sings and plays a number of songs from Scotland. Have a pair of interested students, with help from a music educator, locate an audiocassette, record, or CD that has Scottish songs, to share with the class.

5   The character of the herbalist was based on Rebecca Linkerfelt, whom some thought was a witch. A folktale about her was published in a picture book titled *Heckum Beckum Linkumfelt*. Have a small group of interested students locate a copy of this book and share it with the class.

6   The herbalist showed Valor some of the helpful herbs she used. Some people have favorite "remedies" for various illnesses. Invite a group of students to interview people about home remedies and then share their findings with the class. Discuss whether these remedies seem to be effective, whether they "work" by way of something that can be explained scientifically, or whether they seem to be based on superstition and are without curative value.

 ## Mr. Lincoln's Whiskers

 FICTION

written and illustrated by Karen B. Winnick
Honesdale, PA: Boyds Mills Press, 1996. 32p.

This story will appeal to students in kindergarten through third grade. It contains full-color illustrations.

As the story begins, Grace Bedell, a young girl, runs to meet her father, demanding to know whether he met Mr. Lincoln while he was in New York. She learns that Lincoln had remained in Springfield. As a present, her father gives her a poster of Lincoln, and she comments about his sad face.

At dinner, Grace defends Lincoln because she believes he has a good heart and will try to end slavery. One of her brothers objects, saying that, if elected, Lincoln will divide the country. As Grace is looking at her poster that night, shadows create the illusion that Lincoln has whiskers, which she thinks make his face appear less sad. Quickly, Grace writes a letter to Lincoln, urging him to grow whiskers so that more people will vote for him.

Grace secretly mails the letter. She returns to the post office often, awaiting a reply. On the seventh day, Grace receives a letter from Lincoln. He questions whether it might not appear to be silly affectation if he were to suddenly begin wearing whiskers.

To Grace's delight, Lincoln wins the election. It is reported that he will stop in Westfield, where Grace lives, on his way to inauguration in Washington. Grace goes with her family to the train station where Mr. Lincoln will show her his new whiskers.

Discussion Starters and Multidisciplinary Activities

1 Have students discuss whether they like the appearance of Lincoln better with or without whiskers. Do they think the presence or absence of whiskers would affect voters?

2 Have students discuss why they think Grace kept her letter a secret.

3 Have students discuss how they think Grace must have felt when, during the train stop, Mr. Lincoln asked for her and the people made room for her to approach Mr. Lincoln. What do students think that Grace said to Mr. Lincoln?

4 Have student volunteers sit at a table and role-play their version of the dinner conversation portrayed in the book. One brother thought Lincoln's election would divide the country. Another thought Lincoln was needed because it wasn't fair for one person to own another. Grace and her father were in favor of Lincoln. Have the rest of the class listen to the enactment.

5 If there is a current issue in which students are particularly interested, invite them to write a letter to the president. Mail the letters and share with the class any responses received. (President Bill Clinton, The White House, 1600 Pennsylvania Avenue NW, Washington, DC 20510 or e-mail president@whitehouse.gov.)

6 When Grace wrote her letter to Lincoln in 1860, women did not have the right to vote in the United States. Invite a group of interested students to research this topic. In what year did women gain the right to vote? What action was necessary to give them this right? What individuals were active in the movement for women's rights? Have students share their findings with the class.

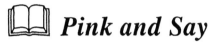 # *Pink and Say*

 FICTION

by Patricia Polacco
New York: Philomel, 1994. 48p. (unnumbered)

This large-format picture book is appropriate for students in kindergarten through third grade when presented by an adult. Death and hardship are depicted. The artwork is bold and bright. This story has been passed down orally from generation to generation.

As the story begins, a black soldier in the Union army comes upon a white Union soldier who has a gunshot wound to the leg. The black soldier explains that they must move, because if they stay in one spot, the Confederate soldiers will find them.

The two soldiers travel a long way on foot, with the black soldier essentially carrying the white soldier most of the way. The black soldier, Pinkus Aylee, called Pink, manages to get the white soldier, Sheldon Curtis, called Say, to the home of his (Pink's) mother, who cares for both. They intend to leave as soon as they can because they are putting Pink's mother in danger.

Pink explains that he and his family are slaves, owned by Master Aylee. He calls slavery "a sickness." Pink served in the Union army in the Forty-eighth division. Say fought in the Ohio Twenty-fourth. Say tells Pink and his mother how he once touched Abraham Lincoln's hand.

As the two soldiers prepare to leave, marauders come. Pink's mother hides them in the root cellar. She is shot and killed. The boys bury her and head for Union army lines, but they are captured and taken to Andersonville Prison. Pink is hanged, but Say remains as a prisoner until he is released some months later and settles in Michigan.

Discussion Starters and Multidisciplinary Activities

1 Neither Say nor Pink really want to return to the fighting. Both are frightened and have suffered. Still, Pink seems more resigned to returning to the fight than Say. Have students discuss this. Is Pink braver than Say?

2 Just before they are captured and sent to Andersonville Prison, Pink gives Say his glasses. Have students discuss why he did this.

3 Have students discuss why it was so important to characters in this story to have "touched the hand that touched the hand" of Abraham Lincoln.

4 Andersonville Prison was real. Have two students, with help from an adult volunteer or a media specialist, research where the prison was located and find the location on a map. Have the students share their findings with the class.

5 This story passed through four generations before it was told to the author of the book. Have interested students trace their own families back four generations and depict this on a "family tree."

6 One of the reasons that Say was "discovered" by enemy soldiers was his accent when he spoke. Ask students and other teachers if they or anyone they know has a "dialect tape," which is often used by actors preparing for a role in the theatre. These tapes contain samples of speech from different regions and parts of the world, such as the northern, western, southern, and eastern United States; Britain; Ireland; and so on. If possible, borrow such a tape and play it for the class.

Reluctant Hero: A Snowy Road to Salem in 1802

FICTION

by Philip Brady
New York: Walker, 1990. 159p.

This book, part of the Walker's American History Series for Young People, will appeal to fourth- and fifth-grade readers. It lacks illustrations. The story is told in the third person from the point of view of 13-year-old Cutting Favour.

The story begins in New Hampshire's hill country in winter. Cutting is driving his oxen on his way to Salem to sell shingles and to purchase supplies for his family, who are starving. With him is his cat, Sam Adams. At an inn, Cutting rescues a young girl, Selina, from the advances of Jake Gurley. The innkeeper decides to send Selina with Cutting, to her family in Salem.

When Cutting and Selina spend the night at Eagle Tavern, Cutting's oxen are stolen. While searching for them, Cutting is shot by someone he doesn't see, but he manages to find his way back to the tavern. Cutting and Selina, fast becoming friends, continue their journey after Cutting has healed. They meet a peddler who tries to trade Cutting some fine carving tools for a cane that Cutting is carving, but Cutting refuses.

Once in Salem, Cutting has trouble selling his shingles, but with Selina's help, he finds a customer. He is nearly robbed but manages to buy supplies and leave a piece of mica with Selina's father for him to sell. He travels partway home with another man, but once he is traveling alone again, Cutting is threatened by Jake Gurley and his companion. Cutting, aided by his cat Sam Adams, injures Jake, drives off Jake's companion, and continues safely on his way.

Discussion Starters and Multidisciplinary Activities

1 Selina proves to be a helpful and resourceful companion. Ask students to point out the many ways in which she assisted Cutting during his mission to Salem.

2 Although Mr. Gilford, the merchant, treated Cutting well and paid a fair price for the walking stick, Cutting was hesitant to ask him about the big piece of mica he'd found. Have students discuss why Cutting hesitated to show the mica to Mr. Gilford.

3 Sam Adams plays a crucial role in this story. Have students discuss the cat and tell what makes this cat so unusual.

4 Have students invite a local woodcarver to visit the class, show carvings, and perhaps demonstrate the woodcarving process. Have the students send an appropriate thank you letter to the guest.

5 Invite a small group of students to research mica. What is it? How is it formed? Where is it commonly found throughout the world? What are its uses? In an oral report, have the students share their findings with the class.

6 Have students test the hardness of various minerals: In a science textbook, find a copy of Mohs' scale of hardness for classifying minerals. Invite students to find various rocks and bring them to class for testing. Can the rock be scratched with a fingernail? With a penny? With a nail? Which rocks are softest? Which are hardest?

 *Wagons West!*

FICTION

written and illustrated by Roy Gerrard
New York: Farrar, Straus & Giroux, 1996. 32p. (unnumbered)

This book, written in verse, will appeal to students in kindergarten through third grade. The author's drawings are in full color and illustrate the pioneers in a distinctive and diminutive style.

The story begins in the 1850s with the arrival of Buckskin Dan, who tells exciting tales about Oregon, 2,000 miles distant. The main character of the story, a young girl, tells how the settlers decided to sell their land, form a wagon train, and follow the trail to Oregon with Buckskin Dan as their guide.

The settlers rendezvous in Independence Town to begin their trip. The wagon train never becomes lost but endures rough weather and hardships. Dan shows the party how to safely float their wagons across the rivers. When the food supply is low, Pa hunts and kills a buffalo. They cross the Platte River and come to Fort Laramie, where they rest, buy provisions, and fix broken gear.

They continue their journey and reach Independence Rock and the Sweetwater River, where they find a lost Arapaho boy named Little Thunder. They bring him along and care for him. Later, they come upon more Arapaho and learn that Little Thunder is the chief's son. To repay the favor for returning Little Thunder, the Arapaho help the settlers when bandits steal their cattle.

The settlers continue. They float rafts down the Columbia River. Finally, they reach the rich farmland of Oregon and begin to turn the Willamette Valley into their new home.

Discussion Starters and Multidisciplinary Activities

1   The art style used in the book is unusual. Have students discuss what they like and dislike about it.

2   Because the people in the wagon train take care of Little Thunder, the Arapaho come to their aid against the bandits. Have students discuss what might have happened if the Arapaho had not come to the settlers' aid.

3   At the end of the story, the reader learns that 20 years have passed since the wagon train arrived in Oregon, and that the little girl has grown up and is now writing her story. Have students discuss the effectiveness of this narrative device.

4   Many history books show the route of the Oregon Trail. Have a pair of students mark the route on a blank map of the United States. They should also mark some of the landmarks along the trail (e.g., Fort Laramie and the Platte River). Display the map in the classroom.

5   When the wagon train stops to rest and obtain supplies at Fort Laramie, the settlers find Native Americans from many tribes involved in trading. Mentioned are Pawnee, Shoshone, Flathead, Cheyenne, Blackfeet, Sioux, Crow, and Arapaho. Invite a group of eight students to research these tribes (one tribe per student) as they were during this time period. How did they dress? In what type of dwellings did they live, and how were the dwellings furnished and decorated? Have the students share their findings with the class.

6   Pa shoots a buffalo when the food supply is low. Have a pair of students research buffalo. What is the average weight of a buffalo? Where do buffalo live today? Have the students share their findings with the class.

Washington City Is Burning   **FICTION**

by Harriette Gillem Robinet

New York: Atheneum Books for Young Readers, 1996. 149p.

This book will appeal to fourth- and fifth-grade readers. It is without illustrations. The story is told in the first person from the point of view of a 12-year-old slave girl, Virginia.

The story begins in 1814 as Virginia rides with Tobias to the president's house to begin working for Dolly Madison. Virginia is already famous among the slaves. To keep secret the fact that slaves had stolen three chickens and were cooking them in a stew, Virginia sat on the cooking pot in the corner, pretending that it was cold. As a result, she burned her legs severely.

A kitten is given to Virginia, and she names it Liberty. At the White House, she learns various duties and makes friends with Pricia and Aunt Sally. Rosetta Bell, another slave, becomes Virginia's enemy.

When there are big parties at the White House, Virginia is called to sneak away, take a carriage, pick up slaves, and drive them to a river, where they escape in boats. In trying to become friends with Rosetta Bell, Virginia foolishly betrays this activity, and as a result, several slaves trying to escape are caught. Virginia continues to help whenever she can.

When the British come, she gives White House clothing to escaping slaves. Rather than escape herself, she remains in Washington with Aunt Sally and Tobias. She intends to remain a slave and continue helping other slaves escape.

Discussion Starters and Multidisciplinary Activities

1   It became clear to the slaves that someone in the White House was betraying them. Ask students whether they were puzzled about the betrayal or if they immediately suspected that Rosetta Bell was responsible.

2   The kitten, Liberty, plays a major role in the story. Have students discuss Liberty's role.

3   Ask students to imagine themselves as being in Virginia's position. What would they have tried to do after the British came to Washington? Would they have remained there? Why?

4   Virginia had scars from being burned with a hot kettle. Invite a school nurse to visit the class and discuss burns. For a mild burn, what is the best procedure to follow? What should be done for serious burns? How can sunburn be avoided?

5   Invite interested students to work together to make a mural picturing the scene after Dolly Madison has left and all the slaves are dressing in fancy clothes and crowding into carriages to escape the city.

6   Several times during the course of the story, characters talk about Benjamin Banneker. Sometimes they call him the "astronomer." Invite a group of students to research Benjamin Banneker and to write a brief report detailing some of his accomplishments. What was his connection with Washington, D.C.? The paper should include a bibliography of sources consulted. Have the students read aloud to the class highlights of their report.

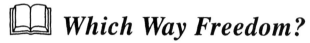 *Which Way Freedom?*

FICTION

by Joyce Hansen
New York: Walker, 1986. 120p.

This book will appeal to fourth- and fifth-grade readers. Except for the cover, the book has no illustrations. The story is told in flashback from the viewpoint of a young black man, Obi, who is 19 at the end of the story.

As the story begins, Obi is a member of the Union army. His good friend Thomas is serving in the army with him. In a flashback, Obi's story is revealed: He is a slave. A girl named Easter and a boy named Jason are also slaves. They are being treated poorly.

Obi decides to escape. An old slave named Buka helps Obi and Easter run toward a river, where they hope to cross to nearby islands. Obi and Easter leave so quickly that they are forced to leave Jason behind.

At the river, they are captured and forced to work for the Confederate army. Buka dies. Easter, dressed as a young boy, cooks and cleans for the colonel. Obi digs trenches and does other work, and becomes friends with Daniel. The two of them decide to make a boat and sail to the closest island.

Obi leaves Easter behind. On the island, Obi trains to become a Union soldier. Daniel is killed. Obi transfers to Tennessee, where he becomes friends with Thomas, who teaches Obi to read.

As the story ends, Obi and Thomas, fighting in the Union army, survive the massacre at Fort Pillow, Tennessee. Obi thinks of the future and hopes that one day he will find Easter and Jason.

Discussion Starters and Multidisciplinary Activities

1 Have students study the dialogue in the book and discuss the mistakes most common in the speech of the slaves. Was the dialogue easy or difficult to understand?

2 Easter never forgave Obi for leaving Jason behind. Have the readers discuss whether Obi did the right thing in refusing to return for Jason.

3 Have students discuss the ending of the story. Why is it so important that Obi get new papers and change his name? Ask students if they think Obi will ever find Easter and Jason.

4 Have a small group of students research the contributions of blacks who fought in the Civil War. Have the group share their findings with the class.

5 *Which Way Freedom?* won the Coretta Scott King Award. Have a pair of students, with help from a media specialist, research this award. How often is it bestowed? Who selects the winner? What sorts of books are eligible for this award? Have the students share what they learn with the class.

6 Have students select one of the 14 chapters in the book and illustrate a significant event from the story. Students may use whatever media they prefer, but they should label each drawing and identify the page where the illustration should be placed. Display the illustrations on a classroom bulletin board.

The 1800s

◆ *Bridges and Poetry* ◆

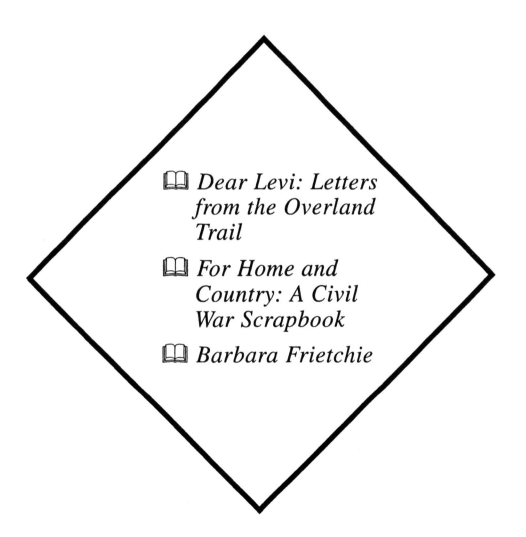

 Dear Levi: Letters from the Overland Trail

 For Home and Country: A Civil War Scrapbook

 Barbara Frietchie

Dear Levi: Letters from the Overland Trail

by Elvira Woodruff
illustrated by Beth Peck
New York: Knopf, 1994.

This bridge book is presented in the form of letters written to a brother in Pennsylvania by a boy traveling the Overland Trail. It will appeal to third- through fifth-grade readers. The book is illustrated with black-and-white pencil sketches.

The main character, Austin, writes to his brother Levi about the adventures that ensue during his 2,500-mile journey to Oregon to reach his father's land claim. Austin travels with the Morrison family.

Austin works at many tasks, including driving the wagon, hunting, and gathering wood. He walks the entire distance because only women and children ride in the wagons. They endure poor weather and sickness, hunger and thirst.

While trading with Native Americans, one of the men in the wagon train, Mr. Hickman, shoots a Native American woman. Frank, Mr. Hickman's son, suffers constant beatings by his father, so he runs away. Several men hunt for him, and this small group is attacked by Native Americans, who kill Mr. Morrison. Austin becomes responsible for the family and does everything he can to help. Mrs. Morrison is expecting a baby. During birth, both Mrs. Morrison and the baby die.

Reuben, a cook, cares for Austin and goes with him to the site of his father's claim. When they learn that the claim has been stolen and sold, Reuben buys it from the new owner. They make plans to settle on the land and hope that Levi will join them.

Possible Topics for Further Investigation

1. Have students make a board game for the class to play: They should prepare several decks of game cards using facts from various disciplines. Each card should pose a question; the back side should reveal the answer. For example, in a deck of math cards, the front of a card might pose the problem $3/4 = ?/8$; the back side would note the answer, $6/8$. Other decks might contain questions about historical figures, places, and dates. Design the playing board (use posterboard) to represent the Overland Trail as a series of squares for moving game pieces. Include squares such as "Native Americans attack," "Broken wagon wheel," "Storm," and so on, to delay the journey (e.g., a player must move back two squares, or skip a turn), as well as squares for speeding the journey (e.g., a player may advance two squares), such as "Hunting is good" or "River is easy to cross." A roll of a die determines how far each player moves if they correctly answer the question on the card. The first player to reach the end wins.

2. Have students, with the help of an adult volunteer or a media specialist, investigate other major trails that settlers used when traveling west, tracing the various routes on a map of the United States. Post the map in the classroom.

3. Using information from the book, have a group of students formulate math problems for the class to solve. For example, if 250,000 people used the Overland Trail to cross the country between 1840 and 1870, and the same number of people used the trail annually, how many used the trail each year? If the distance of 2,400 miles was covered between April 3 and September 8, 1851, how many days did the journey consume? What was the average distance traveled each day?

For Home and Country: A Civil War Scrapbook

by Norman Bolotin and Angela Herb
New York: Lodestar Books, 1995. 98p.

This bridge book is a verbal and pictorial scrapbook of the history of the Civil War. It will be enjoyed by readers in grades three through five.

A time line helps students place into historical perspective some of the major events of the Civil War. The introduction describes the feelings of Thomas Southwick, a 24-year-old New Yorker, and how he is gradually drawn into joining the Union army. He is an example of the many volunteers who hurried to join, fearing the war might end before they enlisted.

An "Outfitting the Troops" section shows different uniforms that were in use and the hardships suffered during the latter part of the war by men lacking shoes and clothing. Although Northern regiments were, for the most part, better supplied than Southern troops, food was often scarce on both sides.

As the Union army marched through the South, the soldiers foraged for food and burned homes. Conditions for the wounded on both sides were terrible. More soldiers died from infection and disease than from battle wounds. Prisoners of war also lived in terrible conditions. Thousands died.

Mail was delivered by train and horse-driven wagon, or carried home by soldiers on leave. Newspaper articles from war correspondents were sent by pony express or telegraph.

After the war, troops came home, black Americans were freed, and the process of reuniting the country began.

Possible Topics for Further Investigation

1   On page 5 of the book is a reproduction of a poster intended to incite volunteers to join the Union army. Invite students to design a poster, using any media, to persuade volunteers to join either the Union army or the Confederate army. Display the posters in the classroom.

2   Page 65 of the book points out that, even during the Civil War, newspapers printed many advertisements in addition to news articles. Invite a group of students to monitor the advertisements in local newspapers for two weeks. Have students clip out advertisements that are unusual in some way (the advertisement itself might be eye-catching, or the advertisement might be for an unusual product). Ask the students to bring these advertisements to class and post them on a classroom bulletin board.

3   In "Battling Boredom," the reader learns that one of the ways Union and Confederate soldiers passed the time while waiting for marching orders was through informal band music. A number of books explain how to make simple musical instruments, such as taping together two Styrofoam cups with rice inside to make a shaker; stretching rubber bands of varying lengths across a board from nail to nail to make a stringed instrument; blowing through a comb covered with waxed paper to make a kazoo; striking bottles containing various levels of water to produce musical tones; and so on. Invite a small group of students to make simple instruments and entertain the class with informal band music.

 *Barbara Frietchie*

by John Greenleaf Whittier
illustrated by Nancy Winslow Parker
New York: Greenwillow Books, 1992. 32p.

BRIDGES AND POETRY

This picture book will appeal to students in kindergarten through third grade. It is illustrated with full-color drawings.

The storyline for this book is the poem "Barbara Frietchie," written by John Greenleaf Whittier. Notes in the book inform the reader that Whittier was an American poet and Quaker. This poem was first published in the *Atlantic Monthly* in 1863. Whittier had heard many firsthand accounts of Barbara Frietchie's actions, which led him to write the poem. As soon as it was published, though, some people denied its historical accuracy.

According to the Frietchie story, in 1862, the second year of the Civil War, citizens of Frederick, Maryland, were evenly divided between loyalty to the Union and sympathy for the Confederacy. Barbara Frietchie was a 95-year-old widow who lived in the town.

When the Confederate troops, led by Stonewall Jackson, arrived on September 10 to march through Frederick, all the American flags that were hanging from buildings were taken down. However, according to the poem, Frietchie hung a Union flag from her upstairs window.

Jackson ordered his troops to fire on the flag. Frietchie grabbed it, waved it out the window, and said, "Shoot, if you must, this old gray head/ But spare your country's flag," she said. The general then ordered the troops not to fire on her, and the Union flag continued to fly throughout the day.

Discussion Starters and Multidisciplinary Activities

1. Have students discuss why, if the people in the town were divided between loyalty to the Union and sympathy with the Confederacy, no one except Barbara Frietchie hung out a Union flag that day.

2. The poem states that when Jackson saw the old woman who dared to fly the Union flag, he felt sadness and shame. Have students discuss this. Why did the general feel these emotions?

3. We don't know if this event really happened, but if it did, how must the citizens of Frederick have felt after the troops had passed through with only one flag waving in the town? Have students discuss this.

4. Excellent pictures of both Union and Confederate flags of the Civil War appear near the beginning and end of the book. Have interested students make copies of these flags using red, white, and blue construction paper. Make a caption for each flag, and post the flags on a classroom bulletin board.

5. This poem might be made into a puppet show, using puppets for General Jackson on horseback, Barbara Frietchie, and a few troops. Have interested students make their puppets and enact the poem as a narrator reads it. Have students share the puppet show with another class.

6. Words selected for use in a poem are different from everyday speech. Invite interested students to write an account of Barbara Frietchie's actions as it might appear the next day in a local newspaper. In class, discuss the differences between the language of the poem and the various newspaper accounts.

The 1800s

Nonfiction Connections

- 📖 *Addy's Cook Book*
- 📖 *Children of the Westward Trail*
- 📖 *Civil War*
- 📖 *Explorers, Trappers, and Guides*
- 📖 *A House Divided: The Lives of Ulysses S. Grant and Robert E. Lee*
- 📖 *Jesse James*
- 📖 *John C. Fremont: Soldier and Pathfinder*
- 📖 *Lewis and Clark: Explorers of the American West*
- 📖 *Matthew Brady: His Life and Photographs*
- 📖 *The Mountain Men*
- 📖 *The Story of Clara Barton*

 **Addy's Cook Book**

edited by Jodi Evert
Middleton, WI: Pleasant, 1994. 44p.

This book will appeal to all elementary-grade students. Included are recipes for meals students can cook today that provide them with insight into dining in the past. Because cooking poses some hazards to young people, adequate adult supervision should be arranged when trying any of the recipes. For each recipe, a list of ingredients and a set of clear directions is provided.

The book begins with a brief sketch of Addy Walker, who escaped to freedom in the North in 1864. Addy went to Philadelphia and brought Southern cooking traditions with her.

In Addy's time, many African Americans lived as slaves on plantations in the South. Slave families were given an allotment of food each week, which they sometimes supplemented by fishing and raising extra vegetables. Many tended gardens on their owner's plantation. They also gathered berries, nuts, and herbs from the nearby woods.

Slave families often cooked their food in small fireplaces in one-room cabins. These fireplaces also provided light. Because a fire was difficult to light, they tried to keep the fire burning constantly. There were no refrigerators, so cooks used their fresh food quickly, before it spoiled. In a slave family's kitchen, the plates and spoons were most likely carved from wood. Bowls might have been made from gourds, and there might have been a few tin cups.

Possible Topics for Further Investigation

1 The book contains a suggestion for a party game, "Novel Writers." Give a sheet of lined paper to one student, who writes a sentence to begin a story. The same student begins a second sentence, but stops in the middle of this sentence, folds over the paper so that only the unfinished sentence can be read, and passes the paper to another student in the class. The second person finishes the sentence, writes another, and then begins another sentence, stopping in the middle. This student folds the paper so that only the unfinished sentence can be read and passes it to a third student. This process continues until everyone has had a turn. Have a student read aloud this most unusual story.

2 Juneteenth is a special celebration that takes place on June 19 in some parts of the country. Have a pair of students research this topic, determine what the celebration commemorates, and share their findings with the class.

3 Have students, with adult supervision, try some of the recipes in the book and serve them at a class party. Some schools have ovens available for class projects. In other cases, home ovens or electric frying pans will be needed. Using some of the recipes suggested for a breakfast might be easy and appropriate: hominy grits, buttermilk biscuits, fried apples, and scrambled eggs would be an enjoyable meal. Have students write thank you letters to those who volunteered food items and those who supervised the cooking.

Children of the Westward Trail

by Rebecca Stefoff
Brookfield, CT: Millbrook Press, 1996. 96p.

This book explores the settlement of western America after the Louisiana Purchase in 1803. It will appeal to fourth- and fifth-grade readers. The illustrations are from historical archives. Much of the information for this book has been obtained from diaries, letters, and journals of pioneer families.

In Chapter 1, the author explains that emigrants went west for many reasons: to seek adventure, to farm, to find gold, to sell goods. By 1869, the railroad was complete, so the journey west became possible for many more people. Many families journeyed west. Martha Gay of Missouri traveled to the Oregon Territory when she was 13. She later wrote of her adventures.

Chapter 2 describes life on the road. Families often took along single men to help with the wagons and livestock. The women cooked the meals and did the laundry. They traveled in covered wagons pulled by teams of oxen. The wagons carried food and a few precious possessions.

Chapters 3 and 4 discuss choosing a route and life in the wagon train. The Santa Fe Trail and the Oregon Trail are described. The Santa Fe Trail, the older of the two, opened in 1821; the Oregon Trail opened in 1841.

Encounters with Native Americans are discussed in Chapter 5. Fewer than one-tenth of all wagon trains were attacked. Chapter 6 tells of the journey's end: Many of the emigrants settled in the Willamette Valley in the Oregon Territory.

Possible Topics for Further Investigation

1. One of the girls' diaries describes how lashing a bucket of milk to the wagon in the morning yields butter by evening. The action of the wagon served to churn the butter. Have a group of students churn butter, with the help of a parent volunteer. Have another group of students and a volunteer bake either bread or biscuits. Allow the class to sample the butter with the bread or biscuits.

2. Invite a group of students to research and determine which trail would be best to take west, and whether they should settle in Oregon or California. In deciding, students should consider the approximate length of the journey, the difficulties that would be encountered, whether a land route would be used all the way or whether water travel would be used part of the way, and what opportunities they would have when the journey ended. Have the students present their data to the class. Have them point out each route using a map, such as the one pictured on page 10 of the book. After the presentation, take a poll of how many classmates were persuaded to follow the route selected by the group.

3. Have a group of students make a relief map using salt and flour, or clay, molded onto a piece of art canvas, showing the various routes between Independence, Missouri, and the West. The map should indicate the Rocky Mountains, the Sierra Nevadas, and the Cascade Range, as well as the Rio Grande, Missouri, and the Colorado rivers. Trails shown should include the Oregon Trail, the California Trail, the Santa Fe Trail, the Old Spanish Trail, and the Gila River Trail. Have the students share their map with the class.

 *Civil War*

by Martin W. Sandler
illustrations from the Library of Congress
New York: HarperCollins, 1996. 91p.

This book will appeal to readers in grades three through five. It is filled with photographs, lithographs, and other illustrative material from the Library of Congress. The book describes the Civil War using excerpts from letters, diaries, and speeches. It also includes some of the first war photographs.

At the heart of the differences that led to war was the fact that the North and South developed in different ways, one with an economy based on factories and the other with an economy based on agriculture. Both sides were confident of a quick victory in war. On both sides, young boys went to war. The Union army had more than 100,000 soldiers under 15 years of age.

The first major battle of the Civil War, the First Battle of Bull Run, was fought in Manassas Junction, Virginia, on July 21, 1861. The casualties numbered 4,878 killed and wounded. The Civil War was also fought at sea. The North had 670 ships to the South's 130 ships. After Fort Sumpter fell, President Lincoln ordered a naval blockade of the South.

Major turning points in the war included the Battle of Gettysburg and the Battle of Vicksburg. General Robert E. Lee finally surrendered to General Ulysses S. Grant on April 9, 1865, at Appomattox. Five days after the surrender, President Lincoln was assassinated.

Possible Topics for Further Investigation

1. With the help of a music educator, locate recordings of songs of the Civil War. Play some of this music for students and discuss it. Among the songs to locate are: "We Are Coming Father Abraham" by James Sloan Gibbons, 1861; "The Bonnie Blue Flag" by Harry Macarthy, 1861; "Dixie" by Albert Pike, c. 1860; "Tenting Tonight on the Old Camp Grounds" by Walter Kittredge, c. 1862; "The Battle Cry of Freedom" by George Frederick Root, c. 1860; and "When Johnny Comes Marching Home" by Patrick Sarsfield Gilmore, 1863.

2. The Civil War marked the first time in history that war was captured by the camera (photography was introduced in 1839). Invite a group of students to research photography. Who were the pioneers in this field? When and what were their contributions? Who was Matthew Brady? Who were Timothy O'Sullivan, Alexander Gardner, George Barnard, and George Cook? Are copies of these photographers' Civil War photographs available in books? Have the students share their findings with the class.

3. Photographs are an effective means of telling a story, especially when combined with writing. Have the class capture the story of your school in words and pictures. Appoint a group of students to research and write the history of the school. This might involve interviewing "old-timers." Appoint another group to capture school scenes with photographs. The final product might be a large scrapbook filled with words and pictures. It might be presented to the school library.

NONFICTION
CONNECTIONS

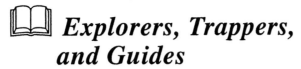 *Explorers, Trappers, and Guides*

by Judith Bentley
New York: Twenty-First Century Books, 1995. 96p.

This book is suitable for readers in grades three through five. It contains black-and-white and color photographs and drawings. Although some of the explorations mentioned in the book occurred before the nineteenth century, the bulk of the book focuses upon the 1800s.

Chapter 1 discusses early explorers who came by sea to reach the Far West. Ships sailed south from Boston or New York, along the coast of South America, headed for Cape Horn, and then went to the northwest coast of the continent. These explorers included Robert Gray, Gabriel Franchere, and Bruno de Hezeta.

Chapter 2 describes encounters along the coast. Europeans, Americans, and coastal Native American tribes met and were both curious and astonished. Fur trading began. Chapter 3 focuses on exploration of the interior. British fur trading companies sent men down rivers from Canada. The United States sent Lewis and Clark to survey the land that the United States had recently purchased from France. In addition to trapping and trading, other explorers, such as David Douglas in the 1820s, documented plant and animal life. His descriptions brought loggers to the Far West.

Chapter 4 details the trapping life. Chapter 5 discusses the contacts and the conflicts that began to arise between explorers and Native Americans. Chapter 6 describes the guides, employed by emigrants and settlers, who established routes to the Far West.

Possible Topics for Further Investigation

1 Have a group of students project and trace onto a large sheet of paper the outline of a map of the United States. Post the map on a classroom bulletin board. Using information from the book as well as from additional research, have the students identify and mark the locations of Native American tribes. Many tribes are discussed in Chapter 5 of the book: Mandan, Sioux, Plains, Blackfeet, Shoshone, Klamath, and Pawnee.

2 Buffalo were slaughtered in the 1880s by white hunters. Efforts have been made to preserve remaining herds in Canada and in the United States. South Dakota is one of the places where buffalo can be found today. Have two students write to the South Dakota Department of Game, Fish, and Parks for information. Or, they might write directly to Custer State Park in the Black Hills of South Dakota (HC 83, Box 70, Custer, SD 57730). The students should request a map and available pamphlets and include a 9-by-12-inch self-addressed envelope stamped with enough return postage for three ounces.

3 Father Junipero Serra is mentioned as one of the early western explorers. He did missionary work with Native Americans in Mexico and then moved to northern California. He founded missions and introduced cattle, sheep, grains, and fruits from Mexico to the California Native Americans. He founded Mission San Diego in 1769, then eight additional missions during his life. Have a small group of interested students research his life. Have them identify on a large map the location of each of Father Serra's missions, noting the founding dates.

A House Divided:
The Lives of Ulysses S. Grant
and Robert E. Lee

by Jules Archer
New York: Scholastic, 1995. 184p.

This book is suitable for fourth- and fifth-grade readers. It contains a few black-and-white photographs.

The first two chapters of the book compare the early lives of Lee and Grant. Lee attended West Point, finishing second in his class, and later married the great-granddaughter of Martha Washington. Grant also attended West Point, graduating in 1843. He married a horsewoman, Julia Dent.

The middle portion of the book discusses the military careers of the two men. Both fought in the Mexican War. After the war, Lee served as superintendent of West Point and later, after his father-in-law died, obtained leave to manage the estate. While on leave, he was summoned to Harpers Ferry.

Grant developed a drinking problem, resigned from the army, farmed unsuccessfully, and began work as a clerk in his brother's leather store.

When the Civil War began, Lee accepted command of the military and naval forces of Virginia and was later promoted to brigadier general of the army of the Confederacy. Grant was appointed colonel of the 21st Illinois volunteers. Later, he was appointed brigadier general in charge of federal troops in Illinois and Missouri. Both became heroes. At Appomattox, Lee surrendered to Grant.

After the war, Lee became president of Washington College in Lexington, Virginia. Grant served two terms as president of the United States, then wrote his memoirs.

Possible Topics for Further Investigation

1 Have interested students research the underlying causes of the war. Was the war fought to abolish slavery? Was the main issue state rights versus the rights of a federal government? Were the main issues economic, pitting the needs and interests of an industrial northern area against those of a primarily agricultural southern area? Was the primary cause for the war related to the threat of possible expansion of slavery into new states? Have five or six students present their views to the class as a panel discussion.

2 Some states clearly supported the Confederacy during the Civil War; some supported the Union. Other states found themselves undecided (people often had relatives fighting in both armies). Invite interested students to make a map of the United States, indicating each state's stance regarding the Civil War. Post the map in the classroom.

3 The book points out how differently Grant and Lee were dressed at Appomattox. Have students play a related observation game: Seat one volunteer in front of the class. Ask another volunteer to study the seated student, paying particular attention to external dress. After two minutes, send the observer out of the classroom. Have the seated volunteer change three things about his/her appearance (e.g., remove a watch, untie a shoe, change the part in the hair, etc.). Have the observer return to the room and try to identify what has been changed.

 # 📖 *Jesse James*

by John Wukovits
Philadelphia: Chelsea House, 1997. 64p.

This book is appropriate for readers in grades four and five. It is part of the Legends of the West series and is illustrated with black-and-white drawings and photographs.

Chapter 1, "Murder at Noon," describes the bank robbery in Gallatin, Missouri, on December 7, 1869, marking the first time Jesse and Frank James committed a robbery on their own. Chapter 2, "Stormy Beginnings," explains why the James family supported the Confederacy during the Civil War even though they lived in Missouri, which remained under Union control. Jesse joined a guerrilla group and was twice wounded.

Chapter 3, "The Making of a Legend," describes Jesse's life of crime. He robbed banks in Missouri and Kentucky and sometimes rode with a gang that included Cole Younger. Chapter 4, "Tell 'em to Come and Get Us," describes how Jesse began robbing trains and stagecoaches. Chapter 5, "Get Your Guns Boys! They're Robbing the Bank," discusses Jesse's robbery of a bank in Minnesota. Many of the gang members were injured.

Chapter 6, "Never Known a Day of Perfect Peace," discusses Jesse and Frank's move to Tennessee to farm. They kept out of sight for three years, but then Jesse began anew, robbing the railroad. A big reward was offered. Jesse moved back to Missouri. Bob Ford, a member of his gang, shot Jesse for the reward money. Frank James surrendered and was tried and acquitted.

Possible Topics for Further Investigation

1 In 1881, a reward of $55,000 was being offered for the capture of the James gang, dead or alive. A picture of the proclamation poster appears on page 37 of the book. Have interested students design posters for the capture of Jesse James. What reward would they offer? What information would they include that would convince people that Jesse James was not a hero but an outlaw?

2 Allan Pinkerton founded the Pinkerton National Detective Agency of Chicago in the 1850s. The group became famous when they uncovered a plot to assassinate President Abraham Lincoln during the Civil War. Invite a group of students to research this agency. What were the agency's more famous cases? What happened to Allan Pinkerton? Have students share their findings with the class.

3 Jesse James was such a legend during his lifetime that many people refused to believe he had been shot. They said that he faked his death and was living elsewhere. In July 1995, a court allowed scientists to dig up the remains of this outlaw and perform genetic tests. These tests confirmed that Jesse James was buried in the grave. With the help of a media specialist, invite two students to use the resources of a local library to locate a newspaper account or magazine account of these tests. Have students share their findings with the class, explaining the steps taken to locate the articles as well.

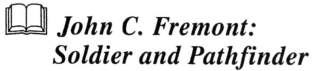 *John C. Fremont:*
Soldier and Pathfinder

by William R. Sanford and Carl R. Green
Springfield, NJ: Enslow, 1996. 48p.

NONFICTION
CONNECTIONS

This book will appeal to readers in grades three through five. It is part of the Legendary Heroes of the Wild West series. The book is divided into nine chapters and is illustrated with black-and-white drawings and photographs.

Fremont was born in Georgia in 1813. He spent some time on the *U.S.S. Natchez* and seemed to be heading for a naval career, but then he was hired to be part of an army survey team. In 1836, he mapped the Carolina woods. He was commissioned as a second lieutenant and assigned to a corps of topographical engineers.

John C. Fremont was nicknamed Pathfinder. In the 1840s, he led four explorations of the lands west of the Rocky Mountains. Fremont made maps of California and Oregon, which allowed pioneers to find their way across the Rockies to the west coast. He met Kit Carson and hired him as a guide. Fremont's wife, Jesse, edited his reports and made them into best-sellers.

On his third expedition, Fremont joined the fight for California's independence. He led troops against landowners in Mexico. General Kearney and Commodore Stockton both gave him orders. Fremont obeyed Stockton, making an enemy of Kearney. He was court-martialed and dismissed from the army. Fremont again headed west. Some of his land proved to be rich in gold.

When California became a state, Fremont was chosen to be one of its first senators. Fremont also ran, unsuccessfully, for president of the United States.

Possible Topics for Further Investigation

1   As a young boy growing up, John Fremont had many patrons. Among them was Joel Poinsett, an important figure in South Carolina. One of the things Poinsett is known for is the introduction into the United States from Mexico of the red Christmas flower that bears his name. Invite a small group of students to research the history of the Poinsettia. Did it have any special significance in Mexico? When and why did Joel Poinsett bring it to the United States? Have the students share what they learn in an oral report to the class.

2   At various times, Fremont spent time at Bent's Fort, Fort Bridger, Fort Vancouver, and Sutter's Fort. Invite four pairs of students to research these four forts. The students should determine the fort's location and its importance in American history, then share this information with the class.

3   Invite to class a person in the community who is skilled in working with topographic maps. Ask this person to bring various topographic maps and teach the students how to read them, so they know how to determine distance from one location to another as well as elevation and differences in elevation. Have the guest pose questions about a specific section of land on specific maps. Students should work in small groups to answer the questions. Have the guest check students' answers. After the visit, have the students send a thank you letter to the guest.

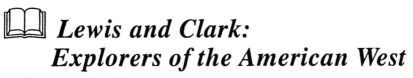

Lewis and Clark: Explorers of the American West

NONFICTION
CONNECTIONS

by Steven Kroll
illustrated by Richard Williams
New York: Holiday House, 1994.

This book is appropriate for second-through fourth-grade students. It is filled with full-page color illustrations.

After President Jefferson sent a minister to arrange with Napoleon the purchase of the land between the Mississippi River and the Rocky Mountains from France for 60 million francs, he asked Captain Meriwether Lewis to lead an expedition to explore the new land. Lewis chose William Clark as coleader. They hoped to open a fur trade, find a water route that would make travel easier across the country, and to learn about the land, animals, and Native Americans.

Clark and his men began traveling up the Missouri on May 14, 1804, in a 55-foot keelboat and two dugout canoes. Lewis joined them, and they reached the mouth of the Platte River on July 21. As they traveled, they met Native Americans and saw animals, such as antelope, prairie dogs, and buffalo.

They wintered at Fort Mandan and were joined by a French Canadian and his Native American wife. In the spring, several men returned to St. Louis, taking samples, maps, and charts to President Jefferson. In late May, the main expedition came upon the Rocky Mountains. They traded goods for horses and traveled over Lost Trail Pass. In dugout canoes, they went down Clearwater River, the Snake River, and the Columbia River, reaching the Pacific Ocean in mid-November. They began their journey home in March and returned to St. Louis on September 23, 1806.

Possible Topics for Further Investigation

1 Page 31 of the book shows important dates of the two-and-one-half-year journey of Lewis and Clark. Have a group of students use this data to create a long, narrow time line for display across one wall of the classroom. The dates should be clearly noted, and students should illustrate the highlights of the journey.

2 Sacagawea is mentioned in this story; she played an important role in the expedition. Ask a pair of students, with the help of a media specialist, to locate other books that have been written about this Native American woman. Have the students share their findings with the class. According to the afterword of the book, opinions differ as to whether Sacagawea died in 1812 of fever or lived until 1884 with the Shoshone in the Far West. Which of these opinions does students' research support?

3 Invite students to imagine that they are part of the Lewis and Clark expedition and have them write seven diary entries. They should try to capture the following: the excitement of beginning the journey; the first sighting of buffalo, antelope, and prairie dogs; the building of a fort and wintering at Fort Mandan; meeting with Native Americans and trading goods with them for needed horses; the first sighting of the Rocky Mountains; reaching the Pacific Ocean; and the cheering along the riverbank when they returned in triumph to St. Louis. Allow time for students to share their diary entries, if desired.

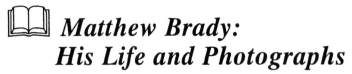

Matthew Brady: His Life and Photographs

by George Sullivan
New York: Cobblehill Books, 1994. 136p.

This book is appropriate for readers in grades four and five. It is illustrated with black-and-white photographs.

Photography was introduced in 1839, so it was relatively new during the Civil War when, for the first time, photographers captured details of battle. Among these Civil War photographers, Matthew Brady is well remembered. In October 1862 in New York, Brady presented an exhibit titled "The Dead at Antietam," the photographs for which were taken by several photographers who worked for Brady.

Brady organized, financed, and supervised teams of photographers and sent them out with the Union forces. He and his photographers also photographed almost every notable American of the time, including presidents, military leaders, and actors.

Brady grew up in Warren County, New York. He became friends with an artist, William Page, and in 1839 went with him to New York City. One of Page's teachers was Samuel Morse, who was both an artist and inventor. Morse was experimenting with the camera. The daguerreotype process was being developed; Brady attended lectures. By 1844, he had opened the Daguerrian Miniature Gallery. In 1888, Eastman introduced the Kodak box camera.

Brady became a photographic historian. He operated a busy portrait gallery but also sold copies of his photographs to anyone who wanted them. He opened multiple galleries in New York and Washington. In spite of successes, Brady spent so much money on photographers and supplies that he went bankrupt.

Possible Topics for Further Investigation

1. Making a pinhole camera is a natural extension for the book: Cut a 1-inch square in the bottom of an empty oatmeal box. Tape a small piece of aluminum foil over the square. Using a fine needle, prick a hole in the middle of the piece of aluminum foil. Tape a piece of tissue paper over the open end of the oatmeal box. On a bright and sunny day, point the pinhole end of the box at a large object, such as a tree across the street. The image will appear upside down on the piece of tissue paper.

2. Queen Victoria opened the first World's Fair in London in 1851. Brady won one of the prizes awarded there for outstanding achievement in photography. Invite a pair of students to research the World's Fairs. In what years and in what places have they been held? What cities in the United States have hosted World's Fairs? Where and when will the next World's Fair be held? Have the students share their findings with the class.

3. Locate a professional or amateur photographer from the community who has a darkroom for printing pictures. Arrange for two or three students who are particularly interested in the process of developing photographs to take a field trip to the photographer's lab and observe printmaking. After the visit, ask the students to share with the class what they saw and learned during their visit. If possible, have them show one or more prints that they helped make.

📖 *The Mountain Men*

by James L. Collins
Danbury, CT: Franklin Watts, 1996. 64p.

This book will appeal to readers in grades three through five. It has color photographs and pictures from historical societies.

Chapter 1 discusses John Coulter (1775–1813), who joined Lewis and Clark's expedition to explore the lands of the Louisiana Purchase. He left the expedition on the trip home, returning to the mountains to live and hunt beaver. He was the first white person to explore what is now Yellowstone National Park. Chapter 2 concerns Manuel Lisa (1772–1820), who, after 1807, averaged one fur trapping expedition a year to trade with the Osage. He established a trading post at the mouth of the Big Horn River in Montana and built a fort there.

Chapter 3 describes Jedediah Smith (1799–1831), who discovered South Pass in what is now the state of Wyoming, and who was the first white person to cross the Sierra Nevadas from west to east. The topic of Chapter 4 is Jim Bridger (1804–1881), who became the first white person to see the Great Salt Lake, and who established Fort Bridger in Wyoming.

In Chapter 5, the reader learns about James Beckwourth (1798–1866), an African American who was adopted into the Crow tribe. Chapter 6 discusses Tom Fitzpatrick (1799–1854), who was a guide and U.S. Indian agent. The book concludes with a discussion of the most famous mountain man, Kit Carson (1809–1868), a hero during the Mexican Indian War and a U.S. Indian agent to the Utes.

Possible Topics for Further Investigation

1 Have a group of students research Yellowstone National Park. They should write to the park service (Superintendent, Yellowstone National Park, P.O. Box 168, Yellowstone National Park, WY 82190) and ask for maps and brochures of the area. Included along with their letter should be a 9-by-12-inch envelope, self-addressed and stamped with sufficient postage for four ounces. Have the students share with the class any materials received, then post the information on a classroom bulletin board.

2 The Great Salt Lake contains 6 billion tons of mineral salt. Have students experiment with the properties of floating objects, comparing tap water to salt water: First, a group of students should use string to tie together wooden coffee stirring sticks to make two rafts. Then they should fill a tub with tap water and a similar tub with tap water in which 1 cup of salt has been dissolved. Put a raft on the tap water, and add small objects until the weight of the objects causes the raft to sink. Put the other raft on the salt water; add the same objects. Does the raft sink in the salt water? Have students explain this phenomenon.

3 In the book are two accounts of mountain men being attacked by bears. These accounts have aspects of tall tales. Invite interested students to write an original account of an experience that a mountain man has with a wild animal. It might be funny or scary. Invite volunteers to read their stories to the class, if desired. Bind the stories together to make a class book. Allow one or more volunteers to illustrate the book.

From *Exploring Our Country's History.* © 1998 Phyllis J. Perry. Teacher Ideas Press. (800) 237-6124.

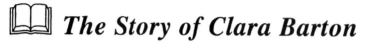

The Story of Clara Barton

NONFICTION
CONNECTIONS

by Zachary Kent
illustrated by Ralph Canaday
Chicago: Childrens Press, 1987. 32p.

This book will appeal to third- and fourth-grade readers. It has black-and-white illustrations and is part of the Cornerstones of Freedom series.

Clara Barton, the youngest in her family, was born on Christmas in 1821. She grew up in Massachusetts. Clara was 11 when her brother fell from a barn roof and was seriously injured. She left school and watched over him day and night.

At age 17, she began teaching; she taught for 10 years. In 1850, she enrolled in Clinton Liberal Institute in New York. She then taught in a private school in Bordentown, New Jersey, and helped establish a public school there.

In 1854, Clara Barton went to Washington, D.C., and worked in the U.S. Patent Office. While in Washington, she heard the arguments about the issue of slavery. As soon as the Civil War began, Clara Barton helped soldiers by collecting supplies and writing to soldiers' families.

At age 40, she received permission to serve as a battlefield nurse. She assisted at Cedar Mountain, the Second Battle of Bull Run, Chantilly, Antietam, Fredericksburg, Morris Island, and Fort Wagner, finally serving as supervisor of nurses for the Union army. After the war, she helped identify soldiers missing in action. During an 1869 trip to England, she learned of the Red Cross. In 1882, Clara Barton became the first president of the American Red Cross.

Possible Topics for Further Investigation

1 Most communities have an American Red Cross office or other agency that offers courses in first aid. In such courses, students learn what to do for various kinds of illnesses and injuries until medical personnel arrive and assume care of the patient. Invite to class someone who is trained in first aid. Ask that person to share with the class information about what to do and what not to do at the scene of an accident. After the visit, have the students send a thank you letter to the guest.

2 Ask a small group of students, with help from a media specialist, to research newspaper articles to determine the major activities of the American Red Cross throughout the country during the past 50 years. The Red Cross may have been called to help with the ravages of floods, tornadoes, earthquakes, and so on. Has it been active in your home state? Have the students write a brief summary of the activities to share with the class.

3 Students who read *The Story of Clara Barton* and other books about Clara Barton will learn what an interesting and varied life she lived while assisting others throughout the world. As a teacher, student, government employee, manager, and (most importantly) nurse, she found ways to help people. Invite students to cut pictures from discarded magazines and use these pictures to create a montage that suggests the life and activities of Clara Barton. Display the montage on a classroom bulletin board.

Part IV

The 1900s

The 1900s

● FICTION ●

- *Alex, Who Won His War*
- *The Bracelet*
- *Don't You Know There's a War On?*
- *Dust for Dinner*
- *Goodbye, Billy Radish*
- *Hard Times: A Story of the Great Depression*
- *Love You, Soldier*
- *Nothing to Fear*
- *Tough Choices: A Story of the Vietnam War*
- *The Unbreakable Code*
- *The Wall*

◆ BRIDGES AND POETRY ◆

- *I Am an American: A True Story of Japanese Internment*
- *Who Shot the President? The Death of John F. Kennedy*
- *Long Ago in Oregon*

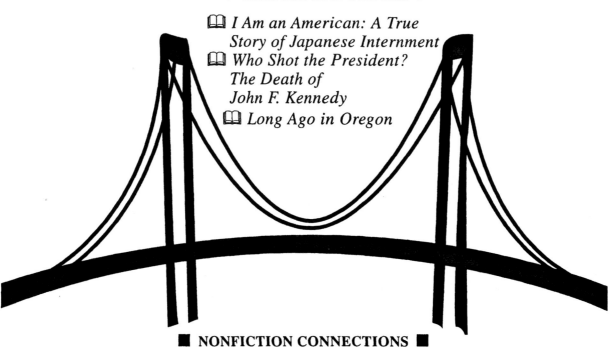

■ NONFICTION CONNECTIONS ■

- *Apollo 11: First Moon Landing*
- *The Dust Bowl: Disaster on the Plains*
- *Franklin D. Roosevelt: A Photo-Illustrated Biography*
- *The Great Depression in American History*
- *Korean War*
- *Martin Luther King, Jr.*
- *The Tuskegee Airmen: Black Heroes of World War II*
- *The Vietnam War: "What Are We Fighting For?"*
- *World War I: "The War to End Wars"*
- *World War II in Europe: "America Goes to War"*
- *World War II in the Pacific: "Remember Pearl Harbor"*

—OTHER TOPICS TO EXPLORE—

—Adolph Hitler	—Eisenhower	—Mussolini	—Progressive Era
—Atom bomb	—Herbert Hoover	—New Deal	—Versailles treaty
—Cold war	—League of Nations	—Panama Canal	—Women's suffrage

From *Exploring Our Country's History.* © 1998 Phyllis J. Perry. Teacher Ideas Press. (800) 237-6124.

● *Fiction* ●

- 📖 *Alex, Who Won His War*
- 📖 *The Bracelet*
- 📖 *Don't You Know There's a War On?*
- 📖 *Dust for Dinner*
- 📖 *Goodbye, Billy Radish*
- 📖 *Hard Times: A Story of the Great Depression*
- 📖 *Love You, Soldier*
- 📖 *Nothing to Fear*
- 📖 *Tough Choices: A Story of the Vietnam War*
- 📖 *The Unbreakable Code*
- 📖 *The Wall*

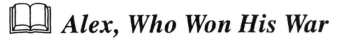 *Alex, Who Won His War*

FICTION

by Chester Aaron
New York: Walker, 1991. 156p.

This book will appeal to fourth- and fifth-grade readers. The central character, Alex Kellar, is 14. The story takes place in Pequod, Connecticut, during World War II.

Alex has a brother, Oliver, who is fighting in the war. Alex has a paper route and sometimes his friend Larry helps deliver the papers. While out on the paper route, the boys find a body on the beach. Before they notify the police, they take the man's wallet. Larry brings the money home to his father, who uses it to buy Christmas presents. Alex immediately begins to fret about the wallet. An article in the paper paints the boys as heroes and the man on the beach as a German spy.

Alex has promised his brother that he will attend to two elderly women on the paper route. Alex goes to see them and learns that two German spies are staying in their home. The spies say that if Alex tells anyone about their presence, they will kill the women.

As a result of the story in the paper, life improves for Larry's family. Family members suddenly find work. The war is going badly, with many losses for the allied forces, and Alex is terrified by the spies, whose secret presence he finally reveals to Larry.

On the day the Germans are to leave, Alex thinks that they will murder him and the two elderly women. At the last moment, Larry comes to the rescue with help. Hans, one of the German spies, tells Alex where the bombs have been planted. The bombs are defused.

Discussion Starters and Multidisciplinary Activities

1. When the story begins, Larry is somewhat an outcast. Have students discuss how Larry changes during the course of the story. What causes these changes?

2. Alex and one of the German spies find themselves drawn together as friends. Have students discuss why Alex feels friendship toward Hans, even though he is a German spy.

3. The bombs that the spies planted as an act of sabotage were due to explode in one hour. Have students discuss Hans's reasons for telling Alex about the bombs?

4. Students may have heard about the Allies and the Axis, but they may not know which countries were on which side during World War II. Invite a pair of students to research this topic and share their findings with the class.

5. Spies sometimes send coded messages. Invite students to write cryptograms—short messages in which one set of letters is substituted for another. The puzzle is solved by examining how often each letter is used and how the letters are grouped. For example, a single letter standing alone must be an *A* or an *I*. Students may want to provide clues for breaking the code, such as N = P or W = U.

6. Hans used an old violin he found in the house to play Haydn's *Emperor Quartet*, or String Quartet in C Major, Opus 76, which became a sort of anthem for Nazi Germany. Have a music specialist play a portion of it for the class and discuss when it was written.

 *The Bracelet*

FICTION

by Hoshiko Uchida
illustrated by Joanna Yardley
New York: Philomel, 1993. 32p. (unnumbered)

This picture book with watercolor illustrations will appeal to students in kindergarten through third grade.

As the story begins, Emi sadly looks around her room, empty like the rest of the house. Presently, she must leave her home and go to the camp where Japanese Americans are being sent, because the United States is at war with Japan. Emi's father is already in a prisoner-of-war camp in Montana because he worked for a Japanese company.

When the doorbell rings, Emi finds her best friend from second grade, Laurie Madison, standing on the doorstep with a good-bye gift. It is a bracelet with a gold heart for Emi to wear to camp.

A neighbor drives Emi and her family to the relocation center, where hundreds of Japanese Americans are gathering. Emi and her mother and sister board buses that will take them to Tanforan Racetrack, which the army has converted into a prison camp. When they reach the camp, they see a barbed wire fence and guard towers.

The family is assigned to a horse stall with three army cots. It is dirty and smelly. After they sweep the stall and set up the cots, Emi notices that her bracelet is missing. They look everywhere but cannot find it.

The next day, as Emi unpacks, she thinks of her friend and her home. She realizes that she doesn't need a bracelet to remember Laurie. She recognizes that even when they are sent to a camp in Utah, Laurie will still be in Emi's heart.

Discussion Starters and Multidisciplinary Activities

1 Although Emi and her relatives are sad, they do not cry as they leave their home and begin life in an internment camp. Have students discuss why this family is so determined not to cry.

2 Although Reiko is angry at the army, which she sees as being stupid and unjust for imprisoning loyal Americans, some people in the story are kind to this Japanese American family. Have students discuss why some citizens were friendly to the family while others didn't trust them and wanted to imprison them.

3 Although Emi's family will be staying in the stables for only a brief time before being moved to a more permanent internment camp, they try to improve their stall. Have students discuss why the family bothers to clean and beautify their temporary surroundings.

4 Ask interested students to imagine themselves as being Emi and write a letter to her best friend, Laurie, about the move to Tanforan Racetrack. Would Emi mention losing the bracelet?

5 Before Emi and her family were sent to an internment camp, they lived in Berkeley, California. Have a small group of students research Berkeley and locate it on a map. For what is the city famous? Have students share their findings with the class.

6 Invite students to supplement the illustrations in the book with a watercolor illustration of their own, identifying the page where the illustration should be placed. Display the illustrations on a classroom bulletin board.

From *Exploring Our Country's History.* © 1998 Phyllis J. Perry. Teacher Ideas Press. (800) 237-6124.

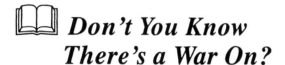 *Don't You Know There's a War On?*

FICTION

by James Stevenson
New York: Greenwillow Books, 1992. 32p. (unnumbered)

This book is illustrated with full-color reproductions of watercolor paintings. It will appeal to students in kindergarten through third grade.

A 10-year-old boy, left at the home front during 1942, narrates. As the book begins, he explains that his brother went into the navy while he stayed at home with his parents.

The boy and others at home try to help win the war. The boy collects tinfoil and rolls it into a ball, saves tin cans, pulls down the shades at night so the enemy won't see lights, and buys war stamps. He helps raise vegetables in a "victory garden" because some food is rationed.

Adults deal with gas rationing. Mr. Halstead serves as an air-raid warden and goes around the neighborhood making sure the houses are blacked out. The boy's friend, Sidney, knows much about war zones throughout the world, and he knows much about military medals. The boy, along with Molly and David, publish a weekly paper called *The Blackout*, which informs readers where they can donate blood and includes recipes that use vegetables from the victory gardens.

One day, the boy's father tells him that he will join the army. When he leaves, the boy keeps a picture of his father in his room. Mother reads the news about the war and worries. When a letter arrives stating that the father has been sent to Florida, the boy and his mother go there for a visit. Finally, the war ends. The boy's brother comes home, and a month later, the boy's father returns.

Discussion Starters and Multidisciplinary Activities

1 The block warden in this story is in charge of making sure that all house lights are out during an air-raid drill. Have students discuss why it would be important to have the town in darkness.

2 The boy saved tinfoil and tin cans. Have students research and discuss this. For what purposes were the foil and tin cans used?

3 When the boy's father leaves to join the army, the boy notices what his father left behind and all the things that are missing. Students may have had similar feelings when a sibling left for summer camp or college, or when a relative left for a vacation. Have students discuss their feelings when being left behind.

4 Sidney knew much about medals. Invite two students, with help from an adult volunteer or a media specialist, to research medals bestowed by the army. They should try to find pictures of such well-known medals as the Bronze Star and the Purple Heart. Have students share with the class what they learn.

5 Guadalcanal is mentioned in the story as a place where fighting occurred during World War II. Ask a pair of students to locate Guadalcanal on a map and research the major battle that was fought there. Have the students share their findings with the class.

6 The boy worked in his victory garden. Students may want to grow vegetables, too. Have students soak seeds overnight and plant them in pots of gardening soil. Carrots, radishes, and pumpkins might be grown. When the seedlings are big enough, allow students to take them home and transplant them to a garden or larger pots.

 *Dust for Dinner*

 FICTION

by Ann Turner
illustrated by Robert Barrett
New York: HarperCollins, 1995.

This beginning reader is suitable for students in kindergarten through second grade. It is part of the I Can Read series, which introduces students to independent reading. Many full-color illustrations are included.

Jake and Maggy live with their parents on a farm. After the area suffers two years of drought and dust storms, the crops fail, and most of the farmers are unable to make a living. They must sell their farms and goods.

An auction is held, and the children are sad to see Mama's rocking chair, their sheep, and the cows sold. Among the few things they save are Mama's radio, their truck, and Sam, the dog. The family gathers its remaining possessions and heads west. Along the way, they stop and try to find work to earn money for food. At one point, Papa finds a job on a farm, but Sam kills one of the farmer's chickens, so again the family must leave.

Times are difficult, and it seems as if the family will be forced to sell Mama's radio, but they manage to keep it. They try to remind themselves that when they reach California, they will have a home again, and they will not eat dust for dinner.

So many people migrate from the Dust Bowl to California that jobs are scarce. Every day, Papa looks for a job, and Mama helps the children with their school lessons. One day, Papa gets a job as a watchman for a big store. He drives Mama and the children to their new house, which has blue shutters and no dust.

Discussion Starters and Multidisciplinary Activities

1. The radio was important in this story. It represented happy times spent as a family, enjoying music and dancing. Discuss with students the fact that television was not available. Have them describe what their family might do in the home for entertainment if television were not available.

2. The author describes a farm auction as being "like a funeral." Have students discuss this. What aspects of the auction were like a funeral?

3. The family faced a dilemma: Stay on a farm and work but get rid of their dog, or leave and hope to find another job. Have students discuss the family's choice.

4. Have a pair of students mark the states of Texas, Oklahoma, Kansas, Colorado, and New Mexico on a map of the United States. Have the students point out these states, the area known as the Dust Bowl, to the class.

5. Pages 50 and 51 of the book describe the family reaching the outskirts of San Francisco and feeling hopeful, but at the same time worried that Papa may not be able to find work. Have four students role-play Papa, Mama, Jake, and Maggy for the class. What might they say to one another as they lie beneath the stars and talk about what the days ahead will bring?

6. Pages 10, 11, 60, and 61 of the book show Mama, Papa, Jake, and Maggy seated around the dinner table. Invite interested students to draw a picture, using any media, showing the family enjoying their first dinner in their new home in California.

From *Exploring Our Country's History*. © 1998 Phyllis J. Perry. Teacher Ideas Press. (800) 237-6124.

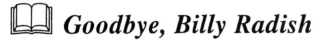 *Goodbye, Billy Radish*

FICTION

by Gloria Skurzynski
New York: Aladdin, 1992. 138p.

This book will appeal to fifth-grade readers. One black-and-white photographic illustration is included per chapter. The central character is 10-year-old Hank Kerner.

Hank lives in Canaan, Pennsylvania. His father and brother, and almost everyone else in the town, work in the steel mill. Hank is afraid of the mill. He has seen men crippled from mill accidents, and he vows he'll never work there. One day, Hank takes his brother's lunch to the mill and witnesses a terrible accident. He fears the mill even more.

Hank makes friends with an immigrant named Bazyli Radichevych, better known as Billy Radish. The two of them grow up together during World War I. As they watch many of the boys and men from Canaan join the war, Hank and Billy wish that they were old enough to serve.

As soon as Billy turns 14, he stops attending school and gets a job in the mill. Hank goes with him one day to see where he works, but Hank is still afraid. The two boys are together for every important event, from spending the Fourth of July to watching Billy's father receive American citizenship.

During an ice storm, Hank helps his sister-in-law deliver a baby. When he goes to tell Billy about the experience and about his dream of being a doctor, he finds Billy gravely ill with the flu. When Billy dies, Hank, also sick with the flu, manages to walk to Billy's funeral. Hank later recovers. He will become a godfather to the new baby who is named Billy.

Discussion Starters and Multidisciplinary Activities

1   Some people might consider Karl to be a coward. Have students cite instances from the text that would support this opinion. At other times, though, he was very brave. Have students quote sections of the book to support this opinion.

2   When Hank went to Billy's name-day celebration, he felt awkward because he couldn't understand what anyone was saying. Ask students to discuss a situation in which they felt out of place. How did they cope with the situation?

3   Billy says that the Ukrainian women have made enough eggs so that the "evil monster is back in chains." He believes this because the war is over and Margie's baby is alive. Yet Billy is dying. Have students discuss this Ukrainian fairytale.

4   Someone in your town or city may have a collection of eggs, including Ukrainian eggs. Invite the collector to visit the class, bring some of their eggs from the collection, and tell a brief story about their history. Have students send a thank you letter to the guest.

5   The author writes that the steel mill in Duquesne, Pennsylvania, has been dismantled. Invite a pair of students to study steel production today. Where are the major steel mills located? How is steel made? Have the students share their findings with the class.

6   Invite interested students to write a Chapter 13 for the book. The date is New Year's Day 1935, and Hank is returning to Canaan to establish his medical practice. Allow students to share their new chapters with the class, if desired.

📖 *Hard Times: A Story of the Great Depression*

● **FICTION**

by Nancy Antle
illustrated by James Watling
New York: Viking, 1993. 54p.

This book will appeal to readers in grades three through five. It contains black-and-white illustrations and is part of the Once Upon America series.

As the story begins, Charlie, a fifth-grader, is talking with his 15-year-old sister, Sally. School is closed in March because there isn't money in Oklahoma to pay teachers or buy supplies. Many people are unemployed. Sally and her husband have moved back home with Sally's parents because they are unable to pay their rent.

Charlie's father arrives home and announces that everyone must move because he has lost his job and can't pay the mortgage. Sally and her husband will go to California. Charlie will move with his sister, Alma, and his parents to his grandparents' home.

As Charlie, Alma, and his parents travel in the truck to the grandparents' home, they become caught in a dust storm. They take shelter with a woman and her child in an old farmhouse. When the storm ends, Charlie's family leaves.

The grandparents are glad to see them. Alma gets a job in the drugstore, Charlie's dad delivers groceries, Charlie's mother helps at church, and Charlie works in the vegetable garden. A hobo named Jim happens by and stays with them. A letter arrives from Sally: She and her husband will return home. When they reach the grandparents' farm, they move in, too. The hope is that next year, things will be better.

Discussion Starters and Multidisciplinary Activities

1. Charlie's harmonica plays a major role in the story. Ask students to discuss the sections of the story in which Charlie plays his harmonica. What function does the harmonica serve in the story?

2. Charlie has a fondness for children. Ask students to point out the sections of the story that show this.

3. Although, by applying to the government, Charlie's father would be eligible for some money to help feed his family, he is very reluctant to do this. Have students discuss his reluctance.

4. This story discusses the Crash of 1929. Invite a group of students to research the crash. What was it? What caused it? What changes and programs were introduced to help prevent another crash like this? Has there been another crash? Have students share with the class what they learn.

5. The man who drove Sally and her husband to Oklahoma from California said that if they would help somebody else, it would be thanks enough. Invite students to write a short story in which Sally and her husband help someone else in need. Allow students to share their stories with the class, if desired.

6. Charlie's father couldn't pay his mortgage. Invite someone who can explain a mortgage to visit the class. Have the guest explain why people have mortgages and how mortgages are paid. Have students send a thank you letter to the guest.

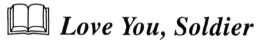 *Love You, Soldier*

FICTION

by Amy Hest
New York: Four Winds Press, 1991. 47p.

This book, without illustrations except for the cover, will appeal to readers in grades two through four. The central character is seven-year-old Katie, whose father is about to join the army.

Katie gives her father a beautiful picture, and the neighbors bid their farewells. In the taxi, driving to the railroad station, Katie's parents hold hands but do not speak. The railroad station is crowded. "Love you, soldier," Katie's mother says as she kisses Katie's father good-bye.

When winter has almost ended, Louise comes to visit. She and Katie's mother were once best friends. Louise's brother and husband are soldiers, too. Louise is expecting a baby, and Katie's mother persuades her to stay with them in New York.

At Passover, Katie and all the people in her building celebrate. Louise's brother Sam comes home on leave for a few days. One day, snow begins to fall, then becomes a blizzard. Louise goes into labor, but Katie's mother is at work. A taxi can't be found, so Katie walks with Louise to the hospital, where Rosie is born.

Months pass. A telegram arrives stating that Katie's father has died in the war. Finally, Louise's husband returns; he takes Louise and Rosie back to Massachusetts. Sam comes home for another visit, then goes to Texas, but he writes often. After the war, he asks Katie and her mother to visit. He and Katie's mother will marry and begin a new life.

Discussion Starters and Multidisciplinary Activities

1. Katie is seven when the story begins and ten when it ends. Have students discuss the ways in which Katie "grew up" during the course of the story. They should cite examples from the text to illustrate Katie's growth.

2. Mrs. Leitstein is "like family." Have students discuss her role in the story. After Katie moves to Texas, will she remember Mrs. Leitstein, write to her, and send pictures?

3. Sam was persistent in writing to Katie. Have students discuss why Sam thought it was so important that Katie be able to write to him and send him a drawing.

4. Young people may not realize that a letter and drawing from them to a distant relative is a precious gift. Encourage students to discuss this at home and bring to class a stamped envelope addressed to an older friend or relative. Have students write letters and draw pictures to mail to older friends or relatives. The letters and pictures might be done in connection with a special holiday greeting.

5. Mrs. Leitstein's cookies were always welcome. Invite a group of students, working with an adult volunteer, to bake cookies, at school or at home, and take them to a senior-citizen retirement home in your community.

6. Invite students to select a favorite scene and draw a full-page illustration using any media, identifying the page where the illustration should be placed. Display the pictures on a classroom bulletin board.

 **Nothing to Fear**

FICTION

by Jackie French Koller

San Diego, CA: Harcourt Brace Jovanovich, 1991. 279p.

This story will appeal to fourth- and fifth-grade readers. Except for its cover, the book has no illustrations. The central character is Danny Garvey, who lives with his mother, father, and baby sister in New York City.

During the Great Depression, almost no one has work. Danny's mother washes clothes. His father finally decides to leave the city and look for work elsewhere. Danny brings home what little money he can from his shoe shining business.

Danny's father does not come home for Thanksgiving or for Christmas, and Danny's mother is pregnant and can't spend much time on her feet. Danny tries to do the washing and ironing, but just as he masters it, he gets fired because the quality of the work has declined.

The people in the apartment building help one another, and Danny is becoming attracted to his spunky neighbor, Maggie Riley. Maggie even shows Danny how to beg for food for his family.

One night, a stranger named Hank arrives sick and penniless on their doorstep. Danny's mother takes him in and nurses him back to health. Hank intends to leave, but through an accident, he finds a good job at the stables. He comes to sleep on the couch at Danny's house and contributes enough money each month to pay the rent. A baby boy is born, but Danny's mother slips into a coma. She survives, and Danny learns that his father was killed by a train on his way home to see them. Eventually, Danny's mother marries Hank, and the four try to establish a new life.

Discussion Starters and Multidisciplinary Activities

1. Danny does not break the grocer's window, but his father holds him responsible for the mischief that was done because he was helping the boys steal candy. As a result, Danny came to know Mr. Weissman well. Have students discuss Mr. Weissman.

2. At the wake, Mickey creates an embarrassing situation for himself by thinking that *taxidermist* is a fancy name for a taxi driver. Have students discuss situations in which they or someone in their family confused one word with another, causing an embarrassing or strange experience.

3. After his mother remarries, Danny keeps his own name. Have students discuss why Danny would want to keep the name of his father and grandfather.

4. Danny accidentally ate a mealworm. Mealworms complete their life cycle in six months and are easy to raise in the classroom. Have students keep mealworms in a container at least 4 inches deep and 10 inches across in 2 inches of oatmeal or bran. Feed the mealworms a slice of apple or potato. Have students observe the life cycle, from mealworm, to pupa, to beetle, to egg.

5. Ask interested students to choose a favorite scene from the book and illustrate it, identifying the page where the illustration should be included. Post the pictures on a classroom bulletin board.

6. Franklin Delano Roosevelt (FDR) was important to Danny and his family. Ask a student to read a biography of FDR and share the highlights of his terms of office orally with the class.

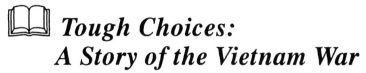 *Tough Choices:*
A Story of the Vietnam War

FICTION

by Nancy Antle
illustrated by Michelle LaPorte
New York: Viking, 1993. 55p.

This story will appeal to readers in grades three through five. It is part of the Once Upon America series and contains black-and-white illustrations.

When the story begins, Samantha, her brother Emmett, her mother, and her brother Mitchell's girlfriend, are hurrying across an airport parking lot to meet a plane. Mitchell, who has been fighting in Vietnam, is coming home on leave. Emmett is opposed to the war, and Samantha worries that he will say something to upset his brother. Anti-war demonstrators are protesting at the airport, and this, too, upsets Samantha. As the group leaves the airport, returning to their car, the demonstrators create a scene as they shout and gather around Mitchell.

The next day, Emmett is making a protest sign to use at a "Die In." Samantha wants to go, but she doesn't want to be disloyal to Mitchell. A car backfire that sounds like a gun sends Mitchell leaping off the bed, reaching for his gun. Samantha goes to watch the Die In and meets an amputee who is watching from the park. The veteran explains that going to war in Vietnam changes one's life.

Mitchell receives a letter from which he learns that his best friend, Jim, was killed the day after Mitchell left Vietnam. Mitchell cuts short his leave. He says that he will not go to the base in North Carolina but instead will stop and see Jim's widow on his way back to Vietnam.

Discussion Starters and Multidisciplinary Activities

1 Samantha is so angry at the airport demonstrators that she wants to stop and hit them. Her brother Emmett would like to protest with them. Ask students to discuss why the sister and brother felt so differently about the demonstrators.

2 Ask students to discuss the Die In. How could such a demonstration be helpful? What harm could it cause?

3 Samantha does not like her brother's girlfriend, Lee Ann. Ask students to point out portions of the story in which Samantha expresses her feelings about Lee Ann. Why does Samantha feel as she does?

4 Samantha wears a POW bracelet. Have a small group of students, with help from a media specialist, research prisoners of war in Vietnam. Were some released? When? Are some still missing? What is being done for those still missing? Have students share their findings with the class.

5 President Lyndon Johnson thought it was important to send troops to Vietnam. Have a group of students research President Johnson. When was he president? What had he done before becoming president? What were his major accomplishments? Have students share their findings with the class.

6 Ask students to play the role of Samantha or Emmett and write a letter to Mitchell just after he cuts short his leave and returns to Vietnam. What news of home might be shared? What words of comfort or advice might be offered? Post the letters on a classroom bulletin board.

 *The Unbreakable Code*

 FICTION

by Sara Hoagland Hunter
illustrated by Julia Miner
Flagstaff, AZ: Northland, 1996. 32p. (unnumbered)

This large-format book with full-color illustrations will appeal to readers in kindergarten through third grade.

As the story begins, John, a Navaho, races up a hill, looking down on Grandfather's farmland. When Grandfather rides up, John explains that he doesn't want to come down and go away to school. Grandfather explains that he'll be okay because he has "an unbreakable code."

In Navajo, Grandfather tells John about attending government school, where they tried to make him forget Navajo. The war began, and when Grandfather enlisted he learned that the marines were looking for men who could speak Navajo. For a successful invasion of the Pacific Islands, ships, planes, and land troops needed effective lines of communication. Because the Japanese had broken all the codes the American forces had used, the marines intended to try Navajo. Because Navajo had not been written down, recruits developed their own code. As Grandfather explains what the Navajo contributed to the war effort, John feels pride, gathers his courage, and is no longer afraid to leave.

An author's note explains that after the bombing of Pearl Harbor on December 7, 1941, President Roosevelt declared war on the Axis powers. Many people joined the armed forces to defend America. Among these were approximately 3,000 Navajo, including 420 "code talkers" who served in the marines.

Discussion Starters and Multidisciplinary Activities

1   John was afraid to leave Grandfather's farm and go away to school. Encourage students to discuss times when they were afraid of new situations. What did they fear? Was the situation as unpleasant as they had expected?

2   What is the nature of the relationship between John and Grandfather? Have students point out details from the story that support their opinions of how the two feel about each other.

3   John refuses to return to school, telling his grandfather, "You don't know what it's like there!" Have students discuss situations at the school that might be causing John to feel so miserable. What could John do?

4   Invite pairs of students, with help from a media specialist, to find books about codes and codebreaking. Have each pair prepare a coded message for the class to decipher.

5   The Navajo chose things from nature to represent letters of the alphabet. For example, *Ant* represented *A*, and *Rabbit* represented *R*. Invite a pair of students to invent a code using words to represent letters of the alphabet, then demonstrate how they can send and receive short messages.

6   An ability to operate radios was a requirement for the Navajo. Invite to class a local amateur radio operator who can bring along a portable rig and who has made arrangements with another local operator to send and receive messages. Have the radio operators demonstrate sending and receiving messages using voice or Morse code. Have students send a thank you letter to each operator.

From *Exploring Our Country's History*. © 1998 Phyllis J. Perry. Teacher Ideas Press. (800) 237-6124.

 *The Wall*

FICTION

by Eve Bunting
illustrated by Ron Himler
New York: Clarion, 1990.

This picture book, with full-color illustrations, will appeal to students in kindergarten through third grade.

A man and his young son go to visit the Vietnam Veterans Memorial in Washington, D.C., which honors the men and women of the armed forces of the United States who served in the Vietnam War. The wall contains more than 58,000 names of those who gave their lives.

The story is told from the viewpoint of the young boy. The boy and his father search for the name of the boy's grandfather. The boy notices that the wall is as shiny as a mirror, reflecting the images of the boy and his father, the trees, and the clouds above them. As they search the wall for Grandpa's name, a man without legs rolls by in a wheelchair. Then the boy sees an old man and woman hugging themselves and crying. He notices all the things that people have brought and left at the wall, including flags, pictures, teddy bears, flowers, and letters.

The boy's father finds the section of the wall that lists the names of men killed in 1967, the year Grandpa died. Finally, he finds the name, George Munoz. The boy's father lifts him up so that he can touch it. The boy's father makes a rubbing of the name. They stand there a long while, and the boy leaves his school picture at the wall. The boy is proud that Grandpa's name is on the wall, but he would rather have Grandpa there with him.

Discussion Starters and Multidisciplinary Activities

1   Ask students if any of them have ever visited the Vietnam Veterans Memorial. If so, have those students describe their visit. If not, share with students magazine or newspaper pictures of the memorial and discuss its significance.

2   Have students discuss the emotions that the boy must have felt when he watched a grandfather and grandson walk by the memorial, talking about walking to the river.

3   The boy's father made a rubbing of Grandpa's name and put it in his wallet. From his wallet, he selected a picture of his son to leave at the wall. Ask students what they can learn about this man based on the contents of his wallet.

4   Some students may want to make a rubbing. Have them make rubbings from a plaque at the school, or from a nearby monument, and share them with the class.

5   The wall is like a mirror, reflecting multiple images. Have a pair of students make a kaleidoscope to demonstrate this effect: Tape together three small mirrors of the same size in a triangular shape, with the mirrored sides facing inward. Stand the mirrors on a piece of waxed paper and trace the triangular outline formed by the mirrors. Cut out the triangle of waxed paper and tape it over the bottom of the kaleidoscope. Cut out many small pieces of colored construction paper and drop them inside the mirrors, then look inside.

6   Invite interested students to write a short poem about the emotions they feel as they look at a picture of the Vietnam Veterans Memorial. Allow students to share their poems with the class, if desired.

The 1900s

◆ *Bridges and Poetry* ◆

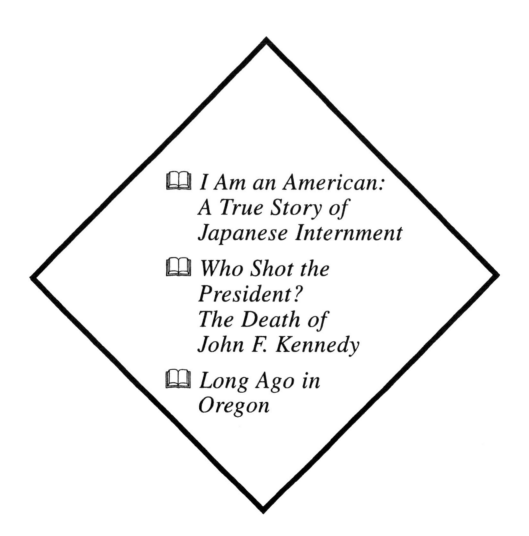

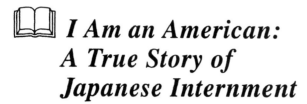

I Am an American: A True Story of Japanese Internment

by Jerry Stanley
New York: Crown, 1994. 102p.

This bridge book is about a Japanese American, Shi Nomura, who was imprisoned by the federal government during World War II. It is based on interviews and personal recollections. The book is illustrated with black-and-white photographs. It will appeal to students in grades four and five.

In 1941, at the time of the attack on Pearl Harbor, Shiro was a senior in high school. Shiro's parents grew fruits and vegetables. Shiro grew up in Keystone, near Los Angeles. After the attack on Pearl Harbor, as the Japanese achieved victories in the Pacific, many people feared the Japanese would invade the west coast of America, and that Japanese Americans would aid them.

In 1942, all Japanese were evacuated from coastal areas and placed in relocation camps. Families had three weeks to prepare for evacuation. Shiro's father sold their farm. The family was then sent by train to Manzanar in the middle of a desert in eastern California. It was one of 10 permanent relocation centers. Shiro's girlfriend was sent to Camp Amache in Colorado.

Because of a shortage of farm laborers, Shiro went to northern Montana to harvest sugar beets. When he returned to Manzanar, the situation had changed. Some had joined the army. Others were furloughed to work. Shiro went to see his girlfriend and then entered a furlough program to work in Denver. Shiro again returned to Manzanar, where he met Mary Kageyama, and they became engaged. On December 17, 1944, the confinement of Japanese Americans ended. Mary and Shiro moved to Pasadena and married in June 1945.

Possible Topics for Further Investigation

1. The introduction of the book discusses the Naturalization Act of 1790, which limited citizenship to "any alien, being a free white person." Have a small group of students research the current naturalization process. How long can people who are not citizens visit in the United States? How can a person born in a foreign country become a U.S. citizen? How long does the process take? Is there a limit on the number of people who may enter the United States from a specific country? Have the students share their findings with the class.

2. The attack on Pearl Harbor in 1941 has been well documented. People who visit Hawaii can take a boat to the USS Arizona Memorial above one of the sunken ships in the harbor. Invite students to research the memorial and battle at Pearl Harbor. When was the memorial built? Over which ship was it built? How many American ships were destroyed during the attack? How many ships were damaged but later returned to service? How many American lives were lost? Have students share their findings with the class.

3. On page 53 of the book is a poster that features Uncle Sam. Invite a pair of students to research Uncle Sam. Who originated this patriotic symbol and when? Have students try their hand at designing an original Uncle Sam poster that might have been used during World War II. Display the posters in the classroom and have students share their findings with the class.

Who Shot the President? The Death of John F. Kennedy

by Judy Donnelly
New York: Random House, 1988. 48p.

This bridge book will appeal to readers in grades two and three. It is illustrated with color photographs and tells a dramatic, true story.

The story begins in Dallas, Texas, on November 22, 1963. President Kennedy and his wife join Texas Governor John Connally and his wife in an open car on their way to a luncheon in their honor. Other cars carry reporters, Secret Service agents, and other important people, such as the Vice President Lyndon Johnson.

They begin a 10-mile trip through the city. A shot rings out; more gunfire follows. Kennedy and Connally are hit. Kennedy is rushed to the hospital; 99 minutes later, Lyndon Johnson is sworn in as president.

The public was fascinated with everything that involved the first family. John Kennedy had been a hero in World War II. His book *Profiles in Courage* won a Pulitzer Prize. Kennedy became a congressman at age 29. Then he was elected senator and, finally, president. He and his wife had young children at the time of his death.

After the assassination, police found bullet shells and a rifle on the sixth floor of the Texas School Book Depository. Lee Harvey Oswald was arrested for the crime. He owned the rifle and worked in the warehouse where the rifle was found. Then Oswald was shot and killed by Jack Ruby. The Warren Commission determined that Oswald, acting alone, shot the president. Many, though, still disagree with that assessment.

Possible Topics for Further Investigation

1 John Kennedy won the Pulitzer Prize for his book *Profiles in Courage*. Have a group of interested students research the Pulitzer Prize. What is it? When is this prize awarded? How often is it awarded? What does it commemorate? Have the students share their findings with the class.

2 Most students will be somewhat familiar with the assassinations of John Kennedy and Abraham Lincoln. They probably will not be as familiar with the killings of James Garfield and William McKinley. Have two small groups of students investigate the killings of Garfield and McKinley. When were they shot? Where were they and what were they doing at the time? Who shot them, and why? Where were Garfield and McKinley buried? Have the groups share with the class what they learn about the assassinations.

3 Although John Kennedy is the most famous member of the Kennedy family, other Kennedys are pictured in the book, and they, too, were involved in American politics. Invite six students to pair together and research the Kennedys. What office did Bobby Kennedy hold, and what happened to him? What office does Ted Kennedy hold, and what part of the country does he represent? Are any of the children of Bobby Kennedy in politics? What positions do they hold? What office does Joseph Kennedy hold, and what part of the country does he represent? Have students share with the class what they learn about the Kennedys.

 *Long Ago in Oregon*

**BRIDGES
AND POETRY**

by Claudia Lewis
illustrated by Joel Fontaine
New York: Harper & Row, 1987. 64p. (unnumbered)

This book of poetry will appeal to elementary students of all ages. The drawings are soft black-and-white sketches.

Although each of the poems in this book stands alone, together they tell the story of a family—a mother, a father, and their five children who live in a small Oregon town during the early 1900s. The poems are written from the point of view of the oldest daughter in the family.

As the book of poems begins, the oldest girl has just finished writing a chapter of a story to be included in a magazine that her brother publishes. It is the year 1917, and her little brothers are outdoors playing "army." She hears her mother and the baby upstairs and leaves to play with her friend.

The girl hopes that Papa will bring a watermelon when he comes home from work. Then in the evening, perhaps they'll take a ride and look upon the valley until it's time to come home to bed.

Other poems are about watching the woodsaw, mother's friend who comes to visit, the farmers and the snakes in the grass, the Nelsons and their store, growing up, Christmas trees, the graveyard on Decoration Day, the new girl at school who hates her mother, the day Milton learned to read, mother's recitation of "The Blue Bird," driving home on a summer day in the Buick, father registering for the draft, Armistice Day, and finally saying good-bye to the old house and moving to Salem.

Discussion Starters and Multidisciplinary Activities

1   After students have read the poems, ask them to examine the illustrations and discuss why each of the pictures is drawn as if slightly out of focus. What effect does this create?

2   When they go to the cemetery on Decoration Day, the grownups talk about veterans of past wars, but the children hunt for graves of other children. Have students discuss this. Why are the children drawn to the graves of other young people?

3   Before moving, the girls in the story take a complete tour of the house. The oldest girl wants to remember as much as she can. Ask students to describe moves that they have made and specific scenes they remember from former homes.

4   Many towns have "historic" or "pioneer" cemeteries. If this is the case where you live, plan a class field trip to such a cemetery, taking time to locate graves of early pioneers and to note the gravestones and their inscriptions. Students might find a year in which several residents died of influenza or in a mine accident. They might note the ages at which the early pioneers died.

5   Using charcoal, pencil, or ink, invite students to make another illustration for the book, identifying the page where the illustration should be placed. Display the drawings on a classroom bulletin board.

6   After students have read the poems, invite them to write a poem about a family enjoying an outing or a holiday. Students may illustrate their poems, if desired. Post the poems on a classroom bulletin board.

From *Exploring Our Country's History.* © 1998 Phyllis J. Perry. Teacher Ideas Press. (800) 237-6124.

The 1900s

■ *Nonfiction Connections* ■

- 📖 *Apollo 11: First Moon Landing*
- 📖 *The Dust Bowl: Disaster on the Plains*
- 📖 *Franklin D. Roosevelt: A Photo-Illustrated Biography*
- 📖 *The Great Depression in American History*
- 📖 *Korean War*
- 📖 *Martin Luther King, Jr.*
- 📖 *The Tuskegee Airmen: Black Heroes of World War II*
- 📖 *The Vietnam War: "What Are We Fighting For?"*
- 📖 *World War I: "The War to End Wars"*
- 📖 *World War II in Europe: "America Goes to War"*
- 📖 *World War II in the Pacific: "Remember Pearl Harbor"*

📖 *Apollo 11: First Moon Landing*

NONFICTION CONNECTIONS

by Michael D. Cole
Springfield, NJ: Enslow, 1995. 48p.

This book will appeal to readers in grades three through five. It is part of the Countdown to Space series and is illustrated with color photographs from the National Aeronautics and Space Administration (NASA).

Chapter 1 describes July 16, 1959. On this day, Michael Collins, Neil Armstrong, and Buzz Aldrin flew to the Moon by way of a Saturn V rocket. Nearly 1 billion people around the world watched the exciting countdown on television.

Chapter 2 describes the four-day trip of 218,986 miles to the Moon. When the third-stage rocket was shut down, the astronauts were in orbit around Earth. After they checked all instruments, they reignited the third-stage rocket, sending themselves at 24,300 miles per hour beyond Earth's gravity on their way to the Moon.

Chapter 3 describes the Moon landing. Aboard the *Eagle*, the lunar module from *Columbia*, Aldrin and Armstrong headed toward the landing site. Armstrong assumed the controls from the automatic landing system and landed in a smooth spot.

Chapter 4 describes the moon walk. Armstrong and Aldrin ate a meal, put on their suits, and climbed down a ladder to the Moon. Neil Armstrong became the first human to step onto the Moon. The astronauts conducted experiments before they returned to the *Eagle*, launched, and docked with *Columbia* in orbit around the Moon.

The return to Earth is the topic of Chapter 5. The astronauts splashed down in the Pacific Ocean two and one-half days later, after leaving an orbit of the Moon.

Possible Topics for Further Investigation

1. The *Apollo 11* mission was an historic accomplishment, but it is only one of a series of space explorations. Divide the class into groups of three or four students each to research space-related topics with the help of a media specialist. Groups might select topics such as the 1997 Mars probe; *Vostok 1*, the first human in space; *Friendship 7*, the first American in orbit; *Columbia*, the space shuttle; *Apollo 13*, space emergency; and *Challenger*, America's space tragedy. Each group should prepare a written report and present the highlights of their report orally to the class.

2. When Neil Armstrong set foot on the Moon, he knew he was being televised and that he was making history. He thought about what he might say as he stepped onto the Moon. His actual words are often quoted: "That's one small step for a man . . . one giant leap for mankind." Ask students to use this statement as they design a poster, in any media, commemorating events in U.S. space exploration. Display the posters on a classroom bulletin board.

3. According to page 32 of the book, the moonwalk created such a sense of awe in CBS television news anchor Walter Cronkite that he was speechless. Ask students to imagine what it would be like to report this event. Invite interested students to write a two-minute description of the Moon landing, practice it, and record it on audiocassette. Have the students play their recording, as if it were a live news broadcast, to the class.

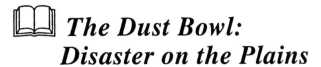

The Dust Bowl: Disaster on the Plains

NONFICTION CONNECTIONS

by Tricia Andryszewski
Brookfield, CT: Millbrook Press, 1993. 64p.

This book will appeal to fourth- and fifth-grade readers. It is part of the Spotlight on American History series, which attempts to place historical events against a backdrop of the people, places, and times that made them possible. The book is illustrated with black-and-white photographs.

By use of a map, the book explains where the Dust Bowl is located. This area of flat or rolling grasslands in Oklahoma, Texas, New Mexico, Colorado, and Kansas usually receives 10 to 20 inches of rain a year, mostly in the spring and fall, and is subject to drought, wind, and prairie fire.

The bison found there supplied food, clothing, and shelter to the Plains Native Americans. Vast groups of prairie dogs also lived in this area. Ranchers and farmers moved there, and the farmers plowed millions of acres of land to plant wheat.

A drought occurred in the 1890s, but the great Dust Bowl drought took place in the 1930s. This was the worst drought to date, lasting from 1931 to 1937. Combined with the crash of the stock market in 1929, it led to the Great Depression. People lost their jobs. Farmers experienced crop failures because of the drought, couldn't pay their bills, and lost their farms. Banks closed. Many people fled to other parts of the country to find work.

The New Deal, working through the Soil Conservation Service, took steps to reclaim the land and prevent a future Dust Bowl from occurring.

Possible Topics for Further Investigation

1 On page 33 of the book are some humorous stories in which the drought and dust are exaggerated. Have students with a sense of humor try to write one of these "tall tales" about the Dust Bowl. Allow students to read aloud their humorous stories, if desired. These stories might be bound into a book for the classroom library.

2 Page 44 of the book shows a color poster published by the Resettlement Administration advertising its services to restore land for its proper use. Another poster on page 37 is from the New Deal's Works Progress Administration and aims to promote confidence in workers. Invite students to research the Civilian Conservation Corps (CCC) and design a poster encouraging people to join the corps. Among other tasks, the corps planted millions of trees to help prevent soil erosion. Display the posters in the classroom.

3 One of the problems still facing residents of the Great Plains is groundwater contamination. Groundwater may be just inches below the soil or may be hundreds of feet deep. Rainwater sometimes carries pollutants into the groundwater. Nitrate contamination and pesticide contamination are two major concerns. Invite a small group of students, working with a media specialist, to research this problem. The United States Environmental Protection Agency (EPA) is reviewing the effects of particular pesticides. Have the students share their findings with the class.

📖 *Franklin D. Roosevelt: A Photo-Illustrated Biography*

NONFICTION CONNECTIONS

by Steve Potts

Mankato, MN: Bridgestone Books, 1996. 24p.

This biography, illustrated with black-and-white photographs, will interest first-through third-grade students.

The book explains that Roosevelt was born to wealthy parents in Hyde Park, New York, where it was common for young children in the 1890s to be taught by tutors. Roosevelt had tutors until he entered Groton School in Massachusetts at age 14. Later, he went to Harvard University and to Columbia University.

In 1905, he married a distant cousin, Eleanor Roosevelt. They raised a daughter and four sons. Eleanor was the niece of President Teddy Roosevelt, a man greatly admired by Franklin Roosevelt. In 1913, Franklin Roosevelt went to Washington, D.C., to serve as assistant secretary of the navy. He continued working there throughout World War I.

In 1920, Roosevelt ran for vice president of the United States on the Democratic Party ticket with James M. Cox. The Democrats lost to the Republicans. In 1921, Roosevelt contracted polio and became paralyzed from the waist down. After four years of treatments, he returned to politics and was elected governor of New York in 1928.

He was elected president in 1932, 1936, 1940, and 1944. The 32d U.S. president, he served longer than any other president, using his New Deal to fight the Great Depression, and leading the United States in becoming a world power during World War II. He died on April 12, 1945.

Possible Topics for Further Investigation

1 Many students will not have known someone who had polio. Have a small group of interested students research polio. What is it? How is it contracted? What is an iron lung? Who invented a vaccine effective against this disease? When did an oral vaccine become common? Do people still receive immunization against this disease? Have the students share their findings by presenting a panel discussion, followed by questions from the class.

2 Invite a pair of interested students to send for additional information about the Franklin D. Roosevelt Library (511 Albany Post Road, Hyde Park, NY 12538) and the Roosevelt Campobello International Park (P.O. Box 97, Lubec, ME 04652). The students should write letters explaining that the class is studying Franklin D. Roosevelt, and request any available pamphlets. Included with each letter should be a self-addressed 9-by-12-inch envelope with enough postage for three ounces for the recipient to use in reply. Have the students share any information received with the class.

3 If the school has access to the World Wide Web, have students investigate web site addresses retrieved by a keyword search on "Franklin D. Roosevelt." Students should print out available material and share it with the class. The following addresses are suggested:

http://www.academic.marist.edu/fdr/frank.htm

http://www.whitehouse.gov/WH/kids/html/kidshome.html

📖 *The Great Depression in American History*

by David K. Fremon
Springfield, NJ: Enslow, 1997. 128p.

**NONFICTION
CONNECTIONS**

This book will appeal to readers in grades four and five. It is illustrated with black-and-white photographs.

Chapter 1 describes how throngs of people gathered in downtown New York on Tuesday, October 29, 1929, in front of the New York Stock Exchange. Many who had lost their investments were waiting to see if they would regain some of their value or go bankrupt. As soon as trading began, it was clear that everyone was selling stock and no one was buying.

Chapter 2 traces America's financial status from the end of World War I to the crash of the stock market. Chapter 3 examines the aftermath of the crash: Banks closed, soup and bread lines formed, many people lost their jobs, and some lost their homes.

In Chapters 4 and 5, the early career and the first term of President Franklin Roosevelt are examined. During his first hundred days in office, Roosevelt used broad executive powers to create dozens of agencies to address problems with agriculture, relief, public works, securities, and unemployment.

The Dust Bowl is discussed in Chapter 6, and the Socialist platform is the topic of Chapter 7. Chapter 8 explores the Second New Deal. Floods, attempts to pack the Supreme Court, a minimum-wage law, the Resettlement Administration, and outlawing child labor were among the issues Roosevelt addressed during this time. Chapter 9 briefly discusses amusements such as sports, radio, and movies enjoyed by people during these difficult times. Chapter 10 provides background for events that led the United States out of the Great Depression and into World War II.

Possible Topics for Further Investigation

1. The most famous book to come out of the Great Depression was John Steinbeck's *The Grapes of Wrath*. Invite a group of students to read and discuss this book. They should choose a section with dialogue and present it as reader's theatre. After the presentation, have the group lead a class discussion on a related topic (e.g., Could our country suffer another depression? What signs forecast a depression?).

2. End Poverty in California (EPIC) was a proposal of Upton Sinclair's for the state to assume control of factories and farms to create goods. Workers would be paid in scrip (paper used as money) to be spent at other EPIC facilities. Have a group of students, with the help of a media specialist, try to locate and photocopy (if copyright allows) articles about this group. Why were they popular? Why did the idea fail? What was their symbol? What techniques were used to ensure that Sinclair would fail in his attempt to win the governorship? Ask the students to share their findings with the class.

3. Roosevelt's Social Security plan in the mid-1920s was, in large part, a move to thwart Francis Townsend's proposal to use a sales tax to accumulate money for senior citizens. Since that time, Social Security has been attacked, supported, and changed many times. If possible, invite someone from a local Social Security office to come to class and explain how the system works, how it is supported, and who is eligible for money. Have students write a thank you letter to the speaker.

 *Korean War*

NONFICTION CONNECTIONS

by Kathlyn Gay and Martin Gay
New York: Twenty-First Century Books, 1996. 64p.

This book will appeal to fifth-grade readers. It is illustrated mainly with black-and-white photographs. The book provides a short but detailed account of the events of the Korean conflict, in seven chapters.

Chapter 1 explains how the dividing line was set at the 38th parallel in Korea after the Japanese surrender in World War II. The Russians were to occupy the northern half of the country and the Americans were to occupy the southern half.

Chapter 2 describes the fall of Seoul and the pouring of well-trained North Korean troops into South Korea. Chapter 3 discusses the response of the United Nations to this invasion. General MacArthur was given permission to establish air and naval support operations around Korea.

Chapter 4 explains the efforts to keep North Korea from taking the port of Pusan and the city of Taegu. Chapter 5 details the surprise amphibious attack on Inchon Harbor. Inchon was captured, and it was a great victory for General MacArthur. Because of this victory, MacArthur wanted to push forward toward the Chinese region of Manchuria. Chapter 6 explains how Chinese troops became involved and sent the American Eighth Army back in retreat.

Chapter 7 discusses the U.S. reaction, peace talks, prisoners of war, and the Korean War Memorial, which was finally dedicated by President Bill Clinton in July 1995.

Possible Topics for Further Investigation

1   In 1952, Dwight Eisenhower was elected president of the United States. Ask a group of students to research Eisenhower. What were the major accomplishments of the Eisenhower administration? What was Eisenhower's profession prior to becoming president? What political party did he represent? Who ran against him during that campaign? What were the main issues of the campaign? What role did Eisenhower play after serving as president of the United States? Have the students share their findings in an oral report to the class.

2   A truce between the United Nations and North Korea was signed on July 27, 1953. South Korea opposed this armistice. Invite a group of students, working with a media specialist, to locate newspaper and magazine accounts of the armistice. They should photocopy (if copyright allows) some of the more interesting of these articles and post them on a classroom bulletin board. Why did South Korea oppose this armistice?

3   General Douglas MacArthur is a controversial figure in American history. He has supporters and detractors both for his service in the Pacific during World War II and for his role in the Korean War. Ask a group of students to research MacArthur and then present a panel discussion for the class in which they explain why some people praise him and some blame him. In preparation, students should research major victories and defeats, as well as the reasons for President Truman's decision to fire him (April 11, 1951).

📖 *Martin Luther King, Jr.*

NONFICTION CONNECTIONS

by Diane Patrick
New York: Franklin Watts, 1990. 64p.

This book is part of the First Books series, suitable for third- through fifth-grade readers. It is illustrated with black-and-white and color photographs.

Martin Luther King Jr. was born January 15, 1929, in Atlanta, Georgia. He excelled in high school and then attended Morehouse College in Atlanta. In his junior year, he became assistant pastor to his reverend at Ebenezer Baptist Church. King studied for his degree in religion at Crozer Theological Seminary in Pennsylvania. He began doctoral studies at Boston University.

King married and became the pastor of the Dexter Avenue Baptist Church in Montgomery, Alabama. Soon, King became the main spokesperson for the blacks involved in the bus boycott. Eventually, the Supreme Court ruled that bus segregation was unconstitutional.

King founded the Southern Christian Leadership Conference (SCLC). When President Kennedy delivered the Civil Rights Bill to Congress, more than 250,000 people came to Washington to demonstrate for its passage. King gave his famous "I Have A Dream" speech. In 1964, he won the Nobel Peace Prize.

In 1965, King led the effort in Selma, Alabama, to remove obstacles to black voter registration. The Voting Rights Act was signed into law by President Johnson in August 1965.

King went to help sanitation workers on strike in Memphis, Tennessee, in February 1968. While there, he was assassinated.

Possible Topics for Further Investigation

1 One of the many awards won by Dr. Martin Luther King Jr. was the Nobel Peace Prize. Ask a small group of students to research this award. Who initiated the award, and why? Who nominates people for the award? Of what does the prize consist? On a chart, have the students list the year and the name and country of the recipient of the award for each of the years it has been awarded.

2 The book discusses several nonviolent protests made by blacks: the Montgomery bus boycott in 1955; the sit-ins at Woolworths in North Carolina in 1960; the 1963 demonstrations in Birmingham, Alabama, leading to the hiring of black workers and desegregation of lunch counters; the August 1963 march on Washington; and the March 1965 march in Montgomery leading to increased black voter registration. Have a group of students, with the help of a media specialist, research these protests, photocopying (if copyright allows) newspaper reports and pictures to share with the class.

3 Many cities and towns hold special celebrations to commemorate Martin Luther King Jr. on the national holiday declared in his honor. Invite students to work with the school principal in planning a special program to be shared at the school on the next Martin Luther King Day. Included might be selections from some of King's famous speeches and writings. A reporter from a local newspaper might be invited to attend the event and write a story.

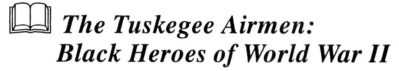 # The Tuskegee Airmen: Black Heroes of World War II

by Jacqueline L. Harris
Parsippany, NJ: Dillon Press, 1996. 144p.

This book will appeal to readers in grades four and five. It is illustrated with black-and-white photographs.

Chapter 1 discusses achievements of early pilots shortly after the Wright brothers pioneered flight in 1903. The first two licensed black pilots, Eugene Bullard and Bessie Coleman, went to France to learn to fly. In the United States, blacks were not admitted to flight schools.

Chapter 2 explains that throughout the 1930s, even those blacks who had completed a civilian-pilot training program were denied entrance in the army air corps. Finally, in 1941, the all-black 99th Pursuit fighter squadron was formed. The men were to be trained at Tuskegee Institute in Alabama. Chapter 3 describes these first black army air cadet pilots. Chapter 4 documents the time in 1943 when black pilots finally went to war, flying many missions over Sicily.

In Chapter 5, the reader learns about three more black squadrons that went to war. The three squadrons of the 332nd Fighter Group—the 100th, the 301st, and the 302nd—arrived on Italy's west coast in February 1944 and soon began escorting bombers as they hit targets in northern France and Germany.

Chapter 6 is devoted to the 477th Bombardment Group. It reveals the racism that these men and their families faced. Chapter 7 discusses the end of segregation in the armed forces because of President Truman's executive order.

Possible Topics for Further Investigation

1 Currently, the United States Air Force Academy is located in Colorado Springs, Colorado. Invite a pair of students to research the Air Force Academy. When was it established? How does one gain admittance to the academy? Have there ever been restrictions to admission to the academy based on race or sex? What is involved in a course of study at the academy? After how many years does one graduate? What rank does the graduate receive? Are pamphlets and pictures of the academy available? Have students share their findings with the class.

2 Although President Harry Truman was able to end segregation in the armed forces in 1948 when he signed Executive Order 9981, various segregation laws were still in effect in many states. Have a group of students, working with a media specialist, research the battle for civil rights that occurred in the United States during the 1950s and 1960s. What were some of the major milestones? By photocopying (if copyright allows) magazine and newspaper stories and pictures, have the students prepare a civil rights display for a classroom bulletin board.

3 Invite an active or retired pilot from the community to visit the classroom. Before the visit, have students prepare questions that they want to ask. A list of these questions should be given to the guest speaker before the visit. After the visit, have students send the pilot a thank you letter.

📖 *The Vietnam War: "What Are We Fighting For?"*

NONFICTION CONNECTIONS

by Deborah Kent
Springfield, NJ: Enslow, 1994. 128p.

This book will appeal to readers in grades four and five. It is part of the American War series and is illustrated with black-and-white photographs. The discussion of the Vietnam War in divided into seven chapters, and the book contains a chronology, notes, suggestions for further reading, and an index.

After Japan's defeat in World War II, Ho Chi Minh assumed control of North Vietnam. Communist forces from North Korea invaded democratic South Korea in 1950. American troops joined the battle and fought to a stalemate. An international conference divided Vietnam at the 17th parallel.

The United States was directly involved in the Vietnam War for 12 years, from 1961 to 1973. Presidents Eisenhower and Kennedy spent millions of dollars to aid non-communist South Vietnam. By 1964, thousands of American military advisors were training and assisting the army of South Vietnam. When it appeared that American ships were being attacked by North Vietnam, President Johnson decided to bomb North Vietnam.

In 1961, U.S. combat troops were sent to Vietnam. North Vietnam received help from the Soviet Union. By 1965, many Americans were protesting against the war. Hundreds of prisoners of war were taken by the Vietnamese. In May 1968, peace negotiations began in Paris. A treaty ending American involvement in the war was signed in January 1973. In 1975, North Vietnam assumed control of the entire country.

Possible Topics for Further Investigation

1 When the Chinese overran Vietnam, the Vietnamese adopted the Chinese form of picture-writing known as calligraphy, although they kept their native language intact. Invite someone who writes in calligraphy to visit the class and demonstrate the techniques, explain the inks and pens used, and describe the various strokes and symbols. After the visit, have a pair of students write a thank you letter to the guest.

2 After the Chinese assumed control of Vietnam, many of the Vietnamese converted to the Chinese Buddhist religion. When the French assumed control of Vietnam, they converted many of the Vietnamese to Catholicism and tried to uproot Buddhism. South Vietnam's prime minister Ngo Dinh Diem was a Catholic. Invite a small group of students to research the Buddhist religion, including its early beginnings and major tenets. Have the students share their findings with the class.

3 After having been under the control of China and France, and after fighting a fierce war, Vietnam became a united and independent nation on May 1, 1975. Students may be interested in learning what has happened to the country since then. Invite a group of students, with the help of a media specialist, to research modern Vietnam. What sort of government exists? Who is its leader? What city is the country's capitol? What are the main industries or agricultural products? Have the students share their findings with the class.

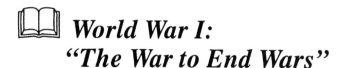 ## *World War I: "The War to End Wars"*

**NONFICTION
CONNECTIONS**

by Zachary Kent
Springfield, NJ: Enslow, 1994. 128 p.

This book will appeal to fifth-grade readers. It is one of eight books in the American War series and is illustrated with black-and-white photographs. The book contains a chronology, a list for further reading, and an index.

The first chapters examine the events leading to the involvement of the United States in World War I. Archduke Franz Ferdinand and his wife were killed on their way to attend a review of Austrian troops in Bosnia. Many Serbs and Croats in Bosnia resented being part of the Hapsburg Empire of Austria-Hungary. This assassination triggered a chain of events. Austria-Hungary declared war on Serbia. Germany declared war on Russia, and on Russia's ally, France. When Germany was denied the right to march through Belgium to attack France,

Belgium's ally, Great Britain, joined the war.

More and more countries became involved in the conflict. Canada, Australia, New Zealand, and India sent troops. The Vietnamese answered France's call for help. Turkey sent troops to help the Germans. Italy declared war against Austria-Hungary. Romania declared war against Austria.

The United States tried to remain neutral, but the sinking of the passenger ship *Lusitania* by a German submarine persuaded our country to declare war against Germany. American troops fought at Belleu Wood, the Marne, and Saint-Mihiel. After Americans assumed control of the Argonne Forest, Germany was crushed. Kaiser Wilhelm II signed the armistice on November 11, 1918.

Possible Topics for Further Investigation

1. One of the figures to emerge as a hero from World War I was Alvin C. York. With seven comrades, Corporal York was able to capture a German battalion, largely because of York's expert marksmanship. He captured 132 prisoners. As a result, York was promoted to sergeant and received many honors. Have a group of students, with the help of a media specialist, research Sergeant York and write a report detailing his heroism to share with the class.

2. President Woodrow Wilson tried to keep our country out of World War I. He has been both praised and criticized for his leadership. After the war, Wilson tried unsuccessfully to persuade Congress to ratify the Treaty of Versailles and to join the League of Nations. Invite a group of six students to research this period in history. Why did some people want the United States to join the League of Nations? Why did others oppose it? As a round-table debate, have three students explain why they support membership in the League while three others present their case for not joining. Follow the debate with a class discussion.

3. Immediately following World War I, American women obtained the right to vote. Invite a group of students to study this period of history. Who were the leading figures in the women's movement? Did World War I further women's rights or hinder the women's movement? Why? Have the students take notes to use in an oral report to the class.

World War II in Europe: "America Goes to War"

NONFICTION
CONNECTIONS

by R. Conrad Stein
Springfield, NJ: Enslow, 1994. 128p.

This book will appeal to fifth-grade readers. It is part of the American War series and is illustrated with black-and-white photographs. The discussion of World War II is divided into seven chapters, and the book contains a chronology, a list for further reading, and an index.

World War II began in Europe when Germany invaded Poland. This caused Britain and France to declare war on Germany. Germany quickly assumed control of Norway and established bases on the North Sea. The Germans attacked France and entered Paris on June 14, 1940.

In April 1941, Germany invaded Greece and Yugoslavia. On June 22, 1941, Hitler invaded Russia. Americans were debating the war when Japan attacked Pearl Harbor on December 7, 1941. America declared war on Japan. Three days later, Germany and Italy declared war on the United States.

America's first troops landed in North Africa. Caught between the Americans and the British, 240,000 German and Italian troops surrendered on May 13, 1943, in Africa. In July 1943, the British and American troops landed at Sicily. At home, the Americans quickly mobilized and, by 1945, had a merchant fleet to send goods and troops to war. D-Day came on June 6, 1944—a fleet carried 200,000 soldiers to the Normandy coast. Days later, the Germans used V-weapons, or buzz bombs.

In the autumn of 1944, German troops launched an offensive called the Battle of the Bulge, but the effort collapsed one month later. On May 7, 1948, Germany surrendered.

Possible Topics for Further Investigation

1   In the early months of World War II, Germany invaded one country after another. Invite a small group of students to draw a large wall map of Europe (they might do this by using an opaque projector to project a map outline onto paper taped to the chalkboard). On their map, they should write the name of each country, and then write the date on which that country was invaded by Germany. Display this map in the classroom throughout the unit of study. This visual chronology will help students understand the spread of the war.

2   While the Nazis were in control of Germany, a terrible period of history known as the Holocaust occurred. Although many people were placed in concentration camps for a variety of reasons, the vast majority of prisoners were Jewish. Invite a group of students to research the Holocaust and the camps at Treblenka, Auschwitz, Berkenau, and others. Ask each of these students to write a paper on some aspect of the Holocaust, citing their sources of information. Post the reports in the classroom.

3   One of the most significant pieces of writing to emerge from this period was *The Diary of Anne Frank*. Anne Frank hid with her family in an attic in Amsterdam. The family was discovered. Anne was sent to a Nazi concentration camp, where she died in 1945. Her diary was published after the war. Invite interested students to read the diary. Allow time for the group to discuss the diary amongst themselves. Have the group decide how to share highlights from this diary and then orchestrate a presentation for the class.

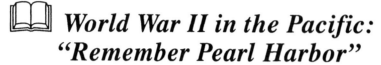 ## *World War II in the Pacific: "Remember Pearl Harbor"*

NONFICTION CONNECTIONS

by R. Conrad Stein
Springfield, NJ: Enslow, 1994. 128p.

This book will appeal to readers in grades four and five. It is part of the American War series and is illustrated with black-and-white photographs. The discussion of World War II is divided into seven chapters and contains a chronology, a list for further reading, and an index.

The book begins with the attack on Pearl Harbor on December 7, 1941. The next day President Roosevelt addressed Congress and asked for and received permission to declare war on Japan. Three days later, Germany and Italy, allied with Japan, declared war on the United States. Japan moved quickly to attack Malaya, Singapore, the Philippines, Guam, and Wake Islands. Thailand, Burma, the Dutch East Indies, and the Solomon and Gilbert Islands were all captured by the Japanese, most within four months of the attack on Pearl Harbor.

In May 1942, Japanese and Americans fought in the Battle of the Coral Sea. They fought at Midway in June 1942. The first U.S. offensive was the landing on Guadalcanal, vital because it held a half-completed airfield.

On the home front, there was tremendous anti-Japanese sentiment. Citizens and aliens of Japanese descent on the west coast were sent to internment camps. Factories and shipyards aided the war effort and used women in the workforce.

The biggest sea battle in history, the Battle of Leyte Gulf, took place in October 1944 and resulted in an American victory. Finally, President Harry Truman ordered that atomic bombs be dropped on Japan. Bombs were dropped on August 6 and 9, 1945. Japan surrendered August 14, 1945.

Possible Topics for Further Investigation

1 Even today, years after World War II, people continue to debate whether the United States should have dropped atomic bombs on Japan. Invite a group of six students, with the assistance of a media specialist, to research the Manhattan Project and the development of the atomic bomb. They should research the scientists who argued against the use of the bomb, the aftermath of the bomb, and the military leaders who thought its use would avert 1 million American casualties. Students should consider as many sources of information as possible, including arguments both for and against the use of this powerful weapon. Have the group debate for the class the dropping of the atomic bombs.

2 In Europe and in the Pacific, tribunals were convened after the end of World War II to investigate war crimes. Many powerful German and Japanese leaders were tried, convicted, and imprisoned or put to death. In some cases, years after the war, Germans were found hiding in South America and brought to trial for their crimes. Have a group of students, with help from a media specialist, investigate these trials and share their findings with the class.

3 Many popular war-related songs were written during World War II. With the help of a music educator, locate audiocassettes, records, or CDs containing such songs and play them for the class. Ask students to listen for elements of humor and nostalgia, and for recurrent themes in the lyrics. Discuss the songs and lyrics.

Part V
ADDITIONAL RESOURCES

📖 Fiction 📖

The 1600s

Accorsi, William. *Friendship's First Thanksgiving*. New York: Holiday House, 1992.

Celsi, Teresa Noel. *Squanto and the First Thanksgiving*. Austin, TX: Raintree Steck-Vaughn, 1992.

Dalgliesh, Alice. *The Thanksgiving Story*. New York: Macmillan, 1987.

Doherty, Brian. *The Story of Pocahontas*. New York: Dover, 1994.

Fleischman, Paul. *Saturnalia*. New York: HarperCollins, 1990.

Fontes, Ron. *Squanto: A Warrior's Tale*. Mahwah, NJ: Troll, 1994.

Gaskin, Carol. *The First Settlers*. New York: Bantam, 1987.

Hooks, William H. *The Legend of the White Doe*. New York: Macmillan, 1988.

Keehn, Sally M. *I Am Regina*. New York: Philomel, 1991.

Montgomery, Raymond A. *Spooky Thanksgiving*. New York: Bantam, 1988.

Smith, Janice Lee. *Turkey Trouble*. New York: HarperCollins, 1990.

The 1700s

Boyd, James. *Drums*. New York: Atheneum, 1995.

Collier, James Lincoln. *War Comes to Willy Freeman*. New York: Dell, 1987.

Durbin, William. *The Broken Blade*. New York: Delacorte Press, 1997.

Edwards, Sally. *George Midgett's War*. New York: Charles Scribner's Sons, 1985.

Hoobler, Dorothy. *The Sign Painter's Secret: The Story of a Revolutionary Girl*. Englewood Cliffs, NJ: Silver Burdett, 1991.

Jensen, Dorothea. *The Riddle of Penncroft Farm*. San Diego, CA: Harcourt Brace Jovanovich, 1989.

Keehn, Sally M. *Moon of the Dark Horses*. New York: Philomel, 1995.

Krensky, Stephen. *The Printer's Apprentice*. New York: Delacorte Press, 1995.

O'Dell, Scott. *Streams to the River, River to the Sea: A Novel of Sacagawea*. Boston: Houghton Mifflin, 1986.

Reit, Seymour. *Behind Rebel Lines*. San Diego, CA: Harcourt Brace Jovanovich, 1988.

Rinaldi, Ann. *Finishing Becca: A Story About Peggy Shippen and Benedict Arnold*. San Diego, CA: Harcourt Brace, 1994.

——. *The Secret of Sarah Revere*. San Diego, CA: Harcourt Brace, 1995.

Rosenburg, John M. *Young George Washington: The Making of a Hero*. Brookfield, CT: Millbrook Press, 1997.

Tripp, Valerie. *Felicity Learns a Lesson: A School Story*. Middleton, WI: Pleasant, 1991.

The 1800s

Armstrong, Jennifer. *The Dreams of Mairhe Mehan*. New York: Alfred A. Knopf, 1996.

Beatty, Patricia. *Who Comes with Canons?* New York: Morrow Junior Books, 1992.

Bohner, Charles. *Bold Journey*. Boston: Houghton Mifflin, 1985.

Denenberg, Barry. *When Will This Cruel War Be Over? The Civil War Diary of Emma Simpson*. New York: Scholastic, 1996.

Donahue, John. *An Island Far from Home*. Minneapolis, MN: Carolrhoda Books, 1995.

Ernst, Kathleen. *The Night Riders of Harpers Ferry*. Shippensburg, PA: White Mane, 1996.

Forrester, Sandra. *Sound the Jubilee*. New York: Lodestar Books, 1995.

Gibboney, Douglas Lee. *Stonewall Jackson at Gettysburg*. Fredericksburg, VA: Sergeant Kirkland's Museum and Historical Society, 1996.

Medearis, Angela Shelf. *Treemonisha*. New York: H. Holt, 1995.

Reeder, Carolyn. *Across the Lines*. New York: Atheneum, 1997.

Rice, James. *Trail Drive*. Gretna, LA: Pelican, 1996.

Smucker, Barbara Claasen. *Selina and the Bear Paw Quilt*. New York: Crown, 1996.

Wisler, G. Clifton. *The Drummer Boy of Vicksburg*. New York: Lodestar, 1997.

The 1900s

Anderson, Rachel. *Paper Faces*. New York: Holt, 1993.

Bartone, Elisa. *American Too*. New York: Lothrop, Lee & Shepard, 1996.

Feder, Paula Kurzband. *The Feather-Bed Journey*. Morton Grove, IL: A. Whitman, 1995.

Hest, Amy. *The Private Notebook of Katie Roberts, Age 11*. Cambridge, MA: Candlewick Press, 1995.

Kinsey-Warnock, Natalie. *The Night the Bells Rang*. New York: Cobblehill Books, 1991.

Manson, Ainslie. *Just Like New*. Toronto: Douglas & McIntyre, 1996.

Mates, Carol. *After the War*. New York: Simon & Schuster, 1996.

Rabin, Staton. *Casey over There*. San Diego, CA: Harcourt Brace Jovanovich, 1994.

Ransom, Candice F. *Jimmy Crack Corn*. Minneapolis, MN: Carolrhoda Books, 1994.

Rinaldi, Ann. *Keep Smiling Through*. San Diego, CA: Harcourt Brace, 1996.

Thesman, Jean. *Molly Donnelly*. Boston: Houghton Mifflin, 1993.

Turnbull, Ann. *Room for a Stranger*. Cambridge, MA: Candlewick Press, 1996.

📖 Nonfiction 📖

The 1600s

Barchers, Suzanne I., and Patricia C. Marden. *Cooking Up U.S. History: Recipes and Research to Share with Children*. Englewood, CO: Teacher Ideas Press, 1991.

Fradin, Dennis B. *The Thirteen Colonies*. Chicago: Childrens Press, 1988.

George, Jean Craighead. *The First Thanksgiving*. New York: Philomel, 1993.

Gourse, Leslie. *Pocahontas*. New York: Aladdin, 1996.

Hayward, Linda. *The First Thanksgiving*. New York: Random House, 1990.

Kallen, Stuart. *Life in the Thirteen Colonies, 1650–1750*. Minneapolis, MN: Abdo and Daughters, 1990.

McGovern, Ann. *If You Lived in Colonial Times*. New York: Scholastic, 1992.

Sakuri, Gail. *The Jamestown Colony*. New York: Children's Press, 1995.

San Souci, Robert. *N. C. Wyeth's Pilgrims*. San Francisco: Chronicle, 1991.

Sewall, Marcia. *The Pilgrims of Plimoth*. New York: Atheneum, 1986.

Smith, Carter, ed. *Daily Life: A Sourcebook on Colonial America*. Brookfield, CT: Millbrook Press, 1991.

Warner, John F. *Colonial American Home Life*. New York: Franklin Watts, 1993.

Waters, Kate. *Samuel Eaton's Day*. New York: Scholastic, 1993.

———. *Sarah Morton's Day*. New York: Scholastic, 1989.

The 1700s

Carter, Alden R. *Darkest Hours*. New York: Franklin Watts, 1988.

Collins, David R. *Casimir Pulaski: Soldier on Horseback*. Gretna, LA: Pelican, 1996.

da Varona, Frank. *Bernardo de Galvez*. Austin, TX: Raintree Steck-Vaughn, 1993.

Egger-Bovet, Howard, and Marlene Smith-Baranzini. *U.S. Kids History: Book of the American Revolution*. Boston: Little, Brown, 1994.

Ford, Barbara. *Paul Revere: Rider for the Revolution*. Springfield, NJ: Enslow, 1997.

Gay, Kathlyn. *Revolutionary War*. New York: Twenty-First Century Books, 1995.

Greenberg, Judith E. *Journal of a Revolutionary War Woman*. New York: Franklin Watts, 1996.

Harness, Cheryl. *Young John Quincy*. New York: Bradbury Press, 1994.

Marrin, Albert. *Struggle for a Continent: The French and Indian Wars, 1690–1760*. New York: Atheneum, 1987.

Meltzer, Milton. *Tom Paine: Voice of Revolution*. New York: Franklin Watts, 1996.

Minks, Louise. *The Revolutionary War*. New York: Facts on File, 1992.

Nardo, Don. *Braving the New World, 1619–1784: From the Arrival of the Enslaved Africans to the End of the American Revolution*. New York: Chelsea House, 1995.

Nordstrom, Judy. *Concord and Lexington*. New York: Dillon Press, 1993.

Old, Wendie C. *George Washington*. Springfield, NJ: Enslow, 1997.

Zeinert, Karen. *Those Remarkable Women of the Revolution*. Brookfield, CT: Millbrook Press, 1996.

The 1800s

Aaseng, Nathan. *From Rags to Riches*. Minneapolis, MN: Lerner, 1990.

Allen, John Logan. *Jedediah Smith and the Mountain Men of the American West*. New York: Chelsea House, 1991.

Alter, Judith. *Growing Up in the Old West*. New York: Franklin Watts, 1989.

Butruille, Susan G. *Women's Voices from the Oregon Trail*. Boise, ID: Tamarack Books, 1993.

Erickson, Paul. *Daily Life in a Covered Wagon*. Washington, DC: Preservation Press, 1994.

Fisher, Leonard Everett. *The Oregon Trail*. New York: Holiday House, 1990.

Fitz-Gerald, Christine Maloney. *Meriwether Lewis and William Clark*. Chicago: Childrens Press, 1991.

Fritz, Jean. *Just a Few Words, Mr. Lincoln: The Story of the Gettysburg Address*. New York: Putnam, 1993.

Levine, Ellen. *If You Traveled on the Underground Railroad*. New York: Scholastic, 1993.

Marrin, Albert. *1812: The War Nobody Won*. New York: Atheneum, 1985.

Moore, Kay. *If You Lived at the Time of the Civil War*. New York: Scholastic, 1994.

Morris, Juddi. *The Harvey Girls: The Women Who Civilized the West*. New York: Walker, 1994.

Murphy, Jim. *The Boys' War*. New York: Clarion Books, 1990.

van Steenwyk, Elizabeth. *The California Gold Rush: West with the Forty-Niners*. Chicago: Watts, 1991.

The 1900s

Black, Wallace, and Jean F. Blashfield. *Island Hopping in the Pacific*. New York: Macmillan, 1992.

Blanco, Richard L. *The Luftwaffe in World War II*. New York: Messner, 1987.

Borden, Louise. *The Little Ships: The Heroic Rescue at Dunkirk in World War II*. New York: Margaret K. McElderry, 1997.

Cooper, Michael. L. *Hell Fighters: African American Soldiers in World War I*. New York: Lodestar, 1997.

Dolan, Edward F. *America in World War I*. Brookfield, CT: Millbrook Press, 1996.

Fincher, E. B. *The Vietnam War*. New York: Franklin Watts, 1980.

Freedman, Russell. *Franklin Delano Roosevelt*. New York: Clarion Books, 1990.

Garland, Sherry. *Vietnam: Rebuilding a Nation*. New York: Dillon Press, 1990.

Humble, Richard. *World War II Aircraft Carrier*. New York: Franklin Watts, 1989.

Nickelson, Henry. *Vietnam*. San Diego, CA: Lucent Books, 1989.

Rice, Earle. *The Attack on Pearl Harbor*. San Diego, CA: Lucent Books, 1997.

——. *The Nuremberg Trials*. San Diego, CA: Lucent Books, 1997.

Stein, R. Conrad. *Hiroshima*. Chicago: Childrens Press, 1987.

📖 Media 📖

Benjamin, Anne. *Young Pocahontas*. Mahwah, NJ: Troll, 1992. 1 book (32p.), 1 audiocassette.

Brenner, Barbara. *Wagon Wheels*. New York: HarperCollins, 1995. 1 book (64p.), 1 audiocassette.

Greene, Carol. *The Pilgrims Are Marching*. Chicago: Childrens Press, 1990. 1 book (29p.), 1 audiocassette. (Sing-along holiday stories.)

Morrow, Honere. *On to Oregon*. Prince Frederick, MD: Recorded Books, 1992. 4 audiocassettes.

O'Dell, Scott. *Sarah Bishop*. Prince Frederick, MD: Recorded Books, 1996. 4 audiocassettes.

Ross, Dana Fuller. *Westward!* Santa Fe, NM: Sunset Productions, 1994. 4 audiocassettes.

Steber, Rich. *Oregon Trail*. Prineville, OR: Bonanza, 1992. 1 audiocassette.

Author, Title, Illustrator Index

About the Author

Phyllis J. Perry has worked as a teacher, an elementary school principal, a district curriculum specialist, a supervisor of student teachers, and as a director of talented and gifted education. She is the author of more than two dozen books for children and teachers including nine First Books for Franklin Watts and the Literature Bridges to Science series for Teacher Ideas Press.

Dr. Perry received her undergraduate degree from the University of California at Berkeley and her doctorate from the University of Colorado in Boulder. She now devotes herself to writing full time and lives with her husband, David, in Boulder, Colorado.